# ON FOREIGN POLICY

# ON POLITICS

*L. Sandy Maisel, Series Editor*

*On Politics* is a new series of short reflections by major scholars on key subfields within political science. Books in the series are personal and practical as well as informed by years of scholarship and deliberation. General readers who want a considered overview of a field as well as students who need a launching platform for new research will find these books a good place to start. Designed for personal libraries as well as student backpacks, these smart books are small format, easy reading, aesthetically pleasing, and affordable.

**Books in the Series**

*On Foreign Policy,* Alexander L. George
*On Thinking Institutionally,* Hugh Heclo

# ALEXANDER L. GEORGE

# ON FOREIGN POLICY
## Unfinished Business

*Paradigm Publishers*
Boulder • London

Published in the United States by Paradigm Publishers, 3360 Mitchell Lane Suite E, Boulder, CO 80305 USA.

Paradigm Publishers is the trade name of Birkenkamp & Company, LLC, Dean Birkenkamp, President and Publisher.

**Library of Congress Cataloging-in-Publication Data**

George, Alexander L.
    On foreign policy : unfinished business / Alexander L. George.
        p. cm. — (On politics)
    Includes bibliographical references and index.
    ISBN 13: 978-1-59451-263-6 (hc)—ISBN 13: 978-1-59451-264-3 (pbk)
    ISBN 1-59451-263-9 (hc : acid-free paper) — ISBN 1-59451-264-7 (pbk : acid-free paper)    1. International relations. 2. International relations—Decision making. 3. United States—Foreign relations. 4. United States—Foreign relations—Decision making. I. Title. II. Series.
    JZ1253.G46 2006
    327.1—dc22

                                2006001596

Printed and bound in the United States of America on acid free paper that meets the standards of the American National Standard for Permanence of Paper for Printed Library Materials.

Designed and Typeset by Hoffman-Paulson Associates

10 09 08 07 06        1 2 3 4 5

# CONTENTS

# INTRODUCTION

I have been perplexed by a number of important puzzles and gaps in studying foreign policy during the course of my career. I have still not been able to deal with them and as I approach the end of my professional career at the age of 85 I hope it is appropriate to write about them in this short book. What better subtitle for it than "Unfinished Business"!

Certainly other scholars have experienced similar or other puzzles and gaps. I hope they, too, will want to share their "unfinished business" with the community of scholars. Publications on international relations and foreign policy do indeed contain evidence of many important disagreements among scholars. But typically what we report in our journals deals mainly with what we, and hopefully others, consider to be progress in developing knowledge and theories. Perhaps too seldom do our journals invite or publish articles that focus instead on important puzzles and gaps. Would editors and those they consult be willing to devote an occasional issue to accounts that focus on puzzles and gaps?

Writing this brief book has provided an opportunity to discuss some of my "unfinished business." But the reader should not expect that the puzzles and gaps discussed in its six chapters will be resolved. They remain, and I hope that others who read this book will be encouraged to address them more effectively than I have been able to do.

What remains in the brief preview of the chapters that follow is to provide some thoughts as to how these puzzles and gaps might be better understood and pursued more effectively.

The reader will note that some of these chapters focus on important conceptual issues. Some key concepts in foreign policy research remain unresolved within the profession; others remain ambiguous or are controversially defined. Several chapters discuss conceptual problems that, ideally, should be resolved before the concepts are converted into variables for detailed research, the various results of which make comparison and cumulation of findings difficult, if not impossible. These concepts, as will be noted, have to do with ideology, national interest, policymakers' judgments, and peace.

Chapter 1 attempts to clarify the concepts of ideology, national interest, and national values. It offers a somewhat novel interpretation of relations among these concepts, challenging some existing formulations. Important questions are left for further study.

Many important puzzles and gaps are ignored or oversimplified. Missing in the literature, for example, is a follow-up to Henry Kissinger's early emphasis on two requirements for dealing with domestic constraints on the conduct of foreign policy. Chapter 2 addresses this question, introducing the concept of "policy legitimacy." A detailed case study is provided that illustrates the relevance of policy legitimacy, which Franklin D. Roosevelt failed to achieve in pursuing his concept of a post–World War II international system. As a result, Roosevelt was forced to settle for a United Nations, which he did not favor.

Writers in the burgeoning literature on "democratic peace" have come to recognize the need to identify different subtypes of "peace." But there is disagreement on the most appropriate subtypes of peace that can contribute to developing sound causal theories. Chapter 3 offers a different set of subtypes of "peace"—precarious peace, conditional peace, and stable peace. This chapter also presents the argument that "democratic peace" is in fact a subtype of "stable peace," one that emerges in relations between states that are not democracies or when only one state is a democracy. Taking "stable peace" into account may facilitate progress in research on "democratic peace."

A major gap in foreign policy analysis is the failure to identify the various types of "judgment" that leaders presumably find it necessary to make in choosing foreign policies. Seven types of judgment are identified in Chapter 4. Only the first is discussed; the other six types remain to be addressed.

The revival of interest in the possible uses of counterfactual analysis—what has often been referred to in the past as "mental experiments"—is addressed and evaluated in Chapter 5. Important requirements for acceptable counterfactual analysis are identified. Under what conditions, then, is rigorous counterfactual analysis a serviceable method? This chapter contributes an answer to this question by providing a case study of inadequate use of counterfactual analysis to support the view that President Woodrow Wilson's stroke in October 1919 explains his gross failure to compromise, as he should have, in order to secure Senate acceptance of the League of Nations.

Another major gap in foreign policy studies is the failure thus far to address the question of how to prevent genocide. Drawing on current, as-yet-unpublished research on this question, Chapter 6 discusses the importance of improving the quality and timeliness of early warning of genocide. It also discusses the need to develop better organization of "warning-response" systems to facilitate policy responses *before* genocide occurs.

*Alexander L. George*

# CHAPTER ONE
# IDEOLOGY, NATIONAL INTEREST,
# AND NATIONAL VALUES

For any hopeful advocate of social
"science" a dip in the cold and murky
waters of the literature on "ideology" is a
shocking and disillusioning experience.
Few concepts in social analysis have
inspired such a flood of commentaries,
yet few have stimulated the production
of so little cumulative knowledge about
society and politics.
                              —Robert Putnam

The difficulty of offering a definition of "ideology" is notorious, and one does so with trepidation. After searching for many years I finally found one that regards political ideology as a set of fundamental beliefs. Ideology is best viewed as a belief system that explains and justifies a preferred political order for society, either one that already exists or one that is proposed.[1] Ideology also offers at least a sketchy notion of strategy (processes, institutional arrangements, programs) for its maintenance or attainment of ideological values. Ideology thus refers in the first instance to a preferred domestic political order, but by extension it may imply or even articulate the notion of a preferred international order as well. This is true particularly, of course, of ideologies that are universalistic rather than particularistic in scope.

It is useful to note that ideology, so defined, is multidimensional: it is essentially a *normative* concept, but it also contains *explanatory* and *prescriptive* dimensions and sometimes also a *predictive* one. The normative component consists of the identification and justification of the preferred order; it sketches but does not develop in detail the features of this preferred order. Coupled with this is an idealized image of the self, actual or potential, with which proponents of the ideology can identify.

The explanatory or analytical component consists of an authoritative diagnosis of the ills and evils of the present political order that is to be replaced by the preferred one (or of a previous political order that has been replaced by the preferred one and/or of an alternative political order that competes with the preferred one). An important feature of the authoritative explanatory-analytical component of ideology is the identification of the enemy.

The prescriptive dimension derives from the fact that ideology is an *action-related* system of ideas; thus ideology implies a commitment to action and contains some notion of a program and at least a general strategy for its realization. In its most virulent form and for those who subscribe to it wholeheartedly, ideology provides a sense of mission and, in foreign policy, an imperative commitment to action.

Finally, when a predictive dimension is also present in ideology, it says or implies something about the prospects for the eventual realization of one's fundamental political values and ideological goals.

It is useful to note that as defined here ideology differs from "political philosophy," which is a disinterested search for the principles of the good state and the good society, and also from "political theory," which is a disinterested search for knowledge of political and social reality.

Having defined political ideology, I shall now discuss the extent to which we can expect "national interest" to discipline and control the impact of ideology on foreign policy in the modern era (as against its ability to have done so in the era of classical European diplomacy).

## The Concept of National Interest

Is the concept of national interest robust enough to enable policymakers, if they are so inclined, to exclude ideological considerations from influencing their foreign policy decisions?[2] Is it possible to discipline the conduct of foreign policy in the modern era in the same way statesmen of the era of classical diplomacy did by adhering to the guidelines of *Realpolitik*? The answers to these questions are negative, and we shall explore why this is so.

## The Realist Approach

Some writers have indeed insisted that national interest is and ought to be separable from ideology. According to this view, it should be possible as well as highly desirable to conduct foreign policy strictly on the basis of sober calculations of the national interest, excluding the "distorting" influence of ideological values, sentiments, and aspirations. This point of view appealed particularly to adherents of the classical Realist approach in the past. For Hans Morgenthau, for example, the national interest was an objective criterion that could and should be applied by statesmen in conducting foreign policy. Moreover, it was asserted that the objective criterion of national interest could also be employed in a "scientific" manner by nongovernment specialists in order to give advice to statesmen and to subject their actions to critical evaluation.

For classical Realists, therefore, national interest was both a normative and a prescriptive concept. In addition, it was employed—for example, via Morgenthau's "rational hypothesis"—for purposes of explaining foreign policy behavior.

The surpassing need to find and use a superordinate criterion such as the national interest is evident. Foreign policy issues typically engage a multiplicity of values and interests that are often difficult to harmonize. Not only is much at stake, but also the various values embedded in the policy problem often pull the decision in different directions. In addition, uncertainty clouds the decisionmaker's judgment as to the benefits to be expected and the likely costs/risks of each of the options he or she is considering.[3]

Under these circumstances it is understandable that the decisionmaker should seek to apply the criterion of national interest in an attempt to cut through the problem of complexity and to cope with the uncertainties affecting choice among alternative policies. A conscientious effort to consider the overall national interest can help to alleviate the psychological malaise an executive experiences in making difficult decisions of this kind. He or she can justify the ensuing decision as one based on careful consideration of the national interest. However, the intellectual guidance the national interest criterion actually gives the decisionmaker in dealing with complex issues is another matter. It is of some importance to understand why this is so.

In the first place, national interest has the characteristics of what decision theorists refer to as a nonoperational goal;[4] it does not provide a measuring rod for comparing policies. National interest is similar in this respect to concepts such as the general welfare and the public interest. Such concepts cannot be employed as a utility function in rigorous policy analysis. They can be related to specific choices of action only through consideration of the subgoals to which they are presumably related. Thus, national interest encompasses subgoals that compete for influence in the conduct of foreign policy. What is lacking is an operational common denominator for dealing with these subgoals. Hence, the relative weight to be given to various subgoals is a matter left to the authoritative (but subjective) judgment of top-level officials.

The limitations of the national interest concept were obscured in an earlier era by simplistic but influential arguments to the effect that national power is the supreme goal of national action. But Realist thinkers who argued this point confused ends and means. However important the acquisition of power, it is in truth a means to an end—security and support for foreign policy goals—and not an end in and of itself. The preoccupation with power, which persists even today, tended to distort the concept of national security, making it appear a simple derivative of power and thereby diverting attention from other prerequisites and strategies for enhancing security and other foreign policy goals.

Further limitations of the national interest concept as a criterion of policy will emerge more clearly if we recall the historical transformation through which the international system has passed. The concept of national interest is associated with the emergence of the nation-state in the sixteenth and seventeenth centuries. The idea of national interest, or *raison d'etat* as it was called, appears to have played a significant role at times in the determination of policy in the classical system of diplomacy before the French Revolution. In this period the national interest was identified with the person of the sovereign, and therefore was unitary and relatively simple to determine.

With the "democratization" of nationalism in the nineteenth century, however, the relative simplicity of the concept of *raison d'état* was eroded, and the state itself came to be seen as composed of different interests. In the era of liberal democracy, "*L'état c'est moi*" was no longer an acceptable answer to the question of sovereign legitimacy. The national interest came to reflect a weighing of various diverse interests within the state, held together, somewhat tenuously at times, by the doctrine of nationalism. It therefore became a more amorphous concept, as different groups within the polity competed to claim it as a legitimizing symbol for their interests and aspirations, which might by no means be shared by many of their compatriots.

With the transition from the laissez-faire to the social service state, the character of the national interest changed further. More groups saw their interests affected by foreign policy, as foreign policy expanded much more deeply and explicitly into the realm of economics. Increasing numbers of individuals and groups asserted interests in, and claims upon, what foreign policy should be. It became more difficult to speak of the state as possessing superior interests of its own that were largely independent of, and transcending, those of its subjects. Thus the scope of national interest was broadened appreciably, in contrast to the situation that prevailed during the nineteenth century.

Moreover, the traditional distinction between "foreign" and "domestic" policy has badly eroded during the past several decades. It has become commonplace now to observe that the most important problems of national policy, such as those having to do with energy, food, inflation, and trade, have both domestic and foreign implications. As a result, the concept of national interest, since it continues to be utilized in determining foreign policy, must encompass the interface between the domestic and foreign sides of the policy issue in question.

Thus, the calculation of national interest has become far more complicated and more unpredictable than it was in the simpler system of classical diplomacy.

If the criterion of national interest has lost much of its earlier utility in providing *guidance* for policymakers, it has become more useful to them in modern times for *justification* of their foreign policy decisions.

Was the foreign policy of a country such as the Soviet Union (or, indeed, that of many other countries) influenced more by policymakers' conceptions of national interest, by their ideology, or by some combination of the two? This question aroused intense controversy among specialists and was not resolved. This would be a difficult question to resolve at best, even if everyone agreed on the definition of these two concepts, because it poses a challenging task for those undertaking rigorous empirical analysis of the motivations contributing to the foreign policy of states.

## The Relation of National Interest to Ideology and National Values

The preceding question along with much of the controversy it generated, it may be noted, presumed that "national interest" and "ideology" are distinct and separable from each other. This assumption, however, is rejected here. To begin with, "national *interest*" is a misnomer; "national *values*" would be a better way of describing what "national *interest*" refers to. The distinction between values and interests is fundamental. "Vital national interests" refer to three fundamental or irreducible national values: (1) the *security and physical survival* of the state (which does not necessarily entail the preservation of all of its territory); (2) the *sovereign inde-*

*pendence and liberty* of the state (which includes the freedom of its inhabitants to choose their own way of life and type of government so as to retain a significant degree of autonomy within the state system); and (3) the maintenance of *economic subsistence* for the populace of the state (i.e., not economic prosperity but, as is fitting for a definition of irreducible national values, a minimal notion of economic well-being.[5]

Given these irreducible national values, "interests" properly defined identify the more specific requirements for preserving these values in different historical contexts and circumstances. Hence, whereas national values can be regarded as permanent and unchanging, unaffected by changes in historical circumstances, interests are in fact context dependent; they can and do change.

To preserve one or another of the fundamental national values, policymakers must decide what interests are relevant and ought to be pursued in foreign and domestic policies. If correctly identified and achieved in reasonable measure, interests are expected to contribute to the three fundamental national values: maintenance of security and physical survival, sovereignty, and economic subsistence. In other words, "interests" are the means to an end and not an end in and of themselves.

The distinction as well as the relationship between a state's fundamental values and possible variations in its foreign policy interests can be easily illustrated. At a certain point in time, given the various historical circumstances that then exist, State A may judge that the preservation of country B's independence is necessary for its own security and physical well-being. The defense of that country is then regarded by State A as among its "vital interests." What this means is that the defense of country B is regarded *under present circumstances* as a means of contributing to State A's fundamental values of security, sovereignty, and/or economic subsistence. The judgment that preservation of another country is in one's own vital interest may indeed persist for some time, but it is essentially context dependent. If a change in circumstances has the effect of reducing the importance of that country to the security of State A and/or of raising the expected costs of defending it to an excessive level, then State A may decide that defense of that country is no longer a vital interest, that other means of ensuring its own security can or should be found.

We can now look more closely at the relationship between ideology and irreducible national values. Ideology (which we have defined as comprising the identification and justification of a preferred political order) is *not* wholly distinct and separable from fundamental national values. Instead the two are linked in that the preferred political order is part of the way of life that makes sovereign independence and liberty one of the irreducible national values.

However, one need not proceed on the assumption that one's own security, way of life, and/or economic subsistence necessarily require that other states share one's ideology, that it is part of one's vital national interests to persuade or coerce other states to adopt a political order and way of life similar to one's own. But that is not to deny that under certain circumstances one's security and/or the safeguarding of one's way of life may be substantially enhanced if other states share one's ideology and have a similar political system, or at least do not subscribe to an antithetical ideology that stimulates mutual hostility. At the same time it must be recognized that even states that share a common ideology can and do have sharp conflicts of interest, stemming from other causes, which can even result in warfare. (One has only to think, in this connection, of the conflict between the Soviet Union and the People's Republic of China and the military action of China against Vietnam.)

This chapter has provided definitions of political ideology, national interest, and national values. It has shown that "national *interest*" is separable from "national *values*" and that "national interests" are context dependent whereas "national values" are not.

There is much of importance that this chapter has not attempted to do. For example, it has left for others the difficult task of empirically assessing the role ideology has played or does play in the foreign policy behavior of different states. And, it has not addressed the important question of how to temper worthwhile ideological aspirations with realism and what specific advice one might give along these lines to policymakers. In brief, there is much "unfinished business" that needs to be addressed.

## Chapter Two
## The Need for
## Policy Legitimacy

The acid test of a policy . . . is its ability
to obtain domestic support. This has two
aspects: the problem of legitimizing a
policy within the governmental appara-
tus . . . and that of harmonizing it with
the national experience.
                                    —Henry Kissinger

The two requirements for achieving domestic support for an ambitious foreign policy identified by
Henry Kissinger encouraged me to develop the concept
of "policy legitimacy," the focus of this chapter. I develop an analytical framework for this purpose, which I use
to analyze Franklin D. Roosevelt's failed effort to develop the kind of policy legitimacy necessary to support
his plan for a cooperative U.S.-Soviet relationship after
the end of World War II.[1]

The forces of public opinion, Congress, the media, and powerful interest groups often make themselves felt in ways that seriously complicate the ability of the president and his advisers to pursue long-range foreign policy objectives in a coherent, consistent manner. It is not surprising that presidents have reacted to these domestic pressures at times by trying to manipulate and control public opinion—as well as to inform and educate the public as best they can.

To be able to do so, the president must achieve a fundamental and stable national consensus, one that encompasses enough members of his own administration, of Congress, and of the interested public. It is contended here that such a consensus cannot be achieved simply by the president adhering scrupulously to constitutional legal requirements for the conduct of foreign policy, *or* by his following the customary norms for consultation of Congress, *or* by his conducting an "open" foreign policy that avoids undue secrecy and deceptive practices, *or* by his attempting to play the role of broker, mediating and balancing the competing demands and claims on foreign policy advanced by the numerous domestic interest groups.

Neither can the president develop such a consensus by invoking the "national interest" or the requirements of "national security." In principle, of course, the criterion of "national interest" should assist the policymaker to cut through the complex, multivalued nature of foreign policy issues and to improve his judgment of the relative importance of different objectives. In practice, however, "national interest" has become so elastic and ambiguous a concept that its role as a guide to foreign policy is highly problematical and controversial. Most thoughtful observers of U.S. foreign policy have long since concluded that the "national interest" concept unfortunately lends itself more readily to being used by our leaders as political rhetoric for *justifying* their decisions and gaining support rather than as an exact, well-defined criterion that enables them to determine what actions and decisions to take.

## The Normative and Cognitive Bases of Policy Legitimacy

A president can achieve legitimacy for his policy only if he succeeds in convincing enough members of his administration, Congress, and the public that he indeed does have a policy and that it is soundly conceived.[2] This requires two things: first, he must convince them that the objectives and goals of his policy are desirable and worth pursuing—in other words, that his policy is consistent with fundamental national values and contributes to their enhancement. This is the *normative* or moral component of policy legitimacy.

Second, the president must convince people that he knows how to achieve these desirable long-range objectives. In other words, he must convince them that he understands other national actors and the evolving world situation well enough to enable him to influence the course of events in the desired direction with the means and resources at his disposal. This is the *cognitive* (or knowledge) basis for policy legitimacy.

Thus, policy legitimacy has both a normative-moral component and a cognitive basis. The normative component establishes the *desirability* of the policy; the cognitive component, its *feasibility*.

Policy legitimacy is invaluable for the conduct of a long-range foreign policy. If the president gains understanding and acceptance of his effort, then the day-to-day actions he takes on its behalf will become less vulnerable to the many pressures and constraints the various manifestations of "democratic control" would otherwise impose on his ability to pursue that policy in a coherent, consistent manner. In the absence of the fundamental consensus that policy legitimacy creates, it becomes necessary for the president to justify each action to implement the long-range policy on its own merits rather than as part of a larger policy design and strategy. The necessity for ad hoc day-to-day building of support under these circumstances makes it virtually impossible for the president to conduct a long-range foreign policy in a coherent, effective manner.

Thus far we have identified the requirements for policy legitimacy in very general terms. In fact, however, the specific operational requirements of normative and cognitive legitimacy will be affected by the marked differences in level of interest and sophistication among individuals and groups. Policy legitimacy must encompass a variety of individuals and groups. Foremost among them are the president and his top foreign policy advisers and officials. It is difficult to imagine them pursuing foreign policy goals that they do not regard as possessing normative and cognitive legitimacy. The bases for their beliefs, however, will not necessarily be communicated fully to all other political actors. In general, as one moves from the highest level of policymaking to the mass public, one expects to find a considerable simplification of the set of assertions and beliefs that lend support to the legitimacy of foreign policy.[3]

## The "Architecture" of Foreign Policy

The knowledge evoked in support of a policy consists of several sets of beliefs, each of which supports a different component of the policy in question. It is useful, therefore, to refine the analytical framework presented thus far in order to understand better the policymaker's task of developing policy legitimacy.

Foreign policy that aims at establishing a new international system or a new set of relationships has an internal structure—a set of interrelated components. These are (1) the *design-objective* of the policy, (2) the *strategy* employed to achieve it, and (3) the *tactics* utilized in implementing that strategy. The choice of each of these components of the policy must be supported by claims that it is grounded in relevant knowledge. A set of plausible cognitive beliefs must support each of the three components of the policy if it is to acquire "cognitive legitimacy."

By taking the internal structure of policy explicitly into account we add a useful dimension to the concept of policy legitimacy. Now the cognitive component of policy legitimacy is analytically differentiated in a way

**The Problem of Achieving Cognitive Legitimacy:**
**The "Internal Structure" of Foreign Policy**
**and Supporting Cognitive Assertions and Beliefs**

| The "Internal Structure" of Foreign Policy | Supporting Cognitive Assertions and Beliefs |
|---|---|
| Choice of (1) Design-Objective | a, b, c, … n |
| Choice of (2) Strategy | a, b, c, … n |
| Choice of (3) Tactics | a, b, c, … n |

that permits a more refined understanding of the task of achieving and maintaining policy legitimacy.

By differentiating the *functional role* that different cognitive assertions and beliefs play in supporting different parts of the internal structure or "architecture" of a policy, the investigator is in a position to do a number of useful things. First, he can understand better the nature of the task a policymaker faces in attempting to achieve legitimacy for his policy. For the policymaker himself to believe that his policy is feasible and to argue this plausibility to others, he has to articulate a set of cognitive beliefs about other national actors whose behavior he seeks to influence and about causal relationships in the issue-area in question that will lend support not only to his choice of the design-objectives of that policy but also to the strategy and tactics that he employs on its behalf.

Second, specification of beliefs supporting the internal structure of a complex foreign policy enables analysts, either at that time or later, to compare these beliefs with the state of scholarly knowledge on these matters. This permits a sharper, better focused evaluation of the validity of the cognitive premises on which different components of a given foreign policy are based.

Third, by keeping in mind the role of cognitive premises, the investigator can more easily refine the description and explanation of pressures for changes in foreign policy that are brought about by interpretations of events that are held to challenge the validity of some of these cognitive premises.

## Roosevelt's "Great Design," Strategy, and Tactics

I shall now utilize the analytical framework outlined above to describe the substance of Roosevelt's postwar policy and to indicate how domestic opinion—and the related need for achieving as much policy legitimacy as possible—constrained Roosevelt's policy choices and his ability to achieve them.

We shall consider first Roosevelt's design-objective for a postwar security system, what he himself called his Great Design. To begin with, the very close connection between Roosevelt's wartime policy and his postwar plans should be recalled. Both were quite self-consciously based on Roosevelt's perception, widely shared by his generation, of the "lessons of the past"—more specifically, the explanations attributed to the various failures of policy after World War I that had led to the rise of totalitarianism and to World War II. Thus, in contrast to the way in which World War I had ended, Roosevelt believed it to be essential this time to completely defeat, disarm, and occupy those aggressor nations that had started World War II. Above all, Roosevelt's planning was dominated by the belief that it was necessary to forestall the possibility that once the war was over the United

States would once again return to an isolationist foreign policy, as it had after World War I.

In short, the postwar objective to which Roosevelt gave the highest priority was to ensure and to legitimize an *internationalist* U.S. postwar foreign policy. He wanted the United States to participate fully and, in fact, to take the lead in efforts to create a workable postwar security system.

To gain public support for his war objectives and to prepare the ground for an internationalist foreign policy thereafter, Roosevelt invoked the nation's traditional idealist impulses and principles. They were written into the Atlantic Charter that he and Churchill agreed to in August 1941 (even before the United States formally entered the conflict), and to which the Russians gave qualified support later.

Thus, the principles of the Atlantic Charter provided *normative* legitimacy for Roosevelt's war aims and his hopes for peace. Among the traditional ideals that Roosevelt invoked, one in particular is of interest here. This was the principle of self-determination and independence for all nations. It was this aspect of the normative legitimacy for his policies that would severely complicate Roosevelt's problems with U.S. public opinion—and President Harry S. Truman's problems later on—when he had to deal with the Russians on matters of territorial settlements and control over Eastern Europe.

Isolationism had been strong in the United States in the 1930s *before* Pearl Harbor. But once the United States got into the war, U.S. opinion developed strong support for the idea that it should not return to an isolationist position. This shift in public opinion was helpful to Roosevelt's postwar plans, but only up to a point, for, in fact, those who opposed a return to isolationism were sharply divided over what type of internationalist policy the United States should pursue after the war. Woodrow Wilson's concept of collective security was revived and its supporters, strong in numbers and influence, wanted the United States to take the lead in establishing a new and stronger League of Nations.

Roosevelt himself, however, rejected this idealist approach as impractical and inadequate. He favored an approach that would take power realities into account. In his view, it was important that the great powers use their military resources to preserve the peace. This would provide a more reliable way than a league for dealing with any new aggressive states that might emerge after the war. Roosevelt also wanted to establish a more effective postwar system than a new league could provide for preventing dangerous rivalries and conflicts from erupting among Britain, Russia, and the United States once the common enemy had been defeated. But Roosevelt did not wish to risk a battle with the Wilsonian idealists, and so he did not publicly articulate his disagreement with their views. Instead he attempted to use their internationalist viewpoint to help legitimate his own quite different version of an internationalist postwar policy.

Roosevelt's thinking about the requirements of a postwar security system was deeply influenced by his awareness of the situation that would confront the peacemakers once the war against the enemy powers was successfully concluded. The defeat of Nazi Germany and its allies would create an important power vacuum in Central Europe. The question of who and what would fill this vacuum would pose the most serious implications for the vital interests of both the Soviets and the Western powers. If the two sides could not cooperate fairly quickly in finding a mutually acceptable approach for dealing with the vacuum in Europe, then they would inevitably enter into the sharpest competition for control of Central Europe.

The resulting dangers to the peace, it would be foreseen, could be dealt with only within the framework of the existing alliance between the Western powers and the Soviet Union. There would be no other international forums or institutions to bring into play to regulate competition among the victorious powers over Central Europe. Whatever semblance of an international system that had existed in the period between the two world wars had collapsed. What is more, the military alliance between the Western powers and the Soviet Union had been forced on them by circumstances—the common danger of defeat and domination by Nazi Germany and its allies. Once the enemy powers were defeated, all of the long-standing differences in ideology and the historic lack of trust and mutual suspicion between the West and the Soviet Union would have an opportunity to emerge once again.

Roosevelt was aware that once the wartime alliance achieved its purpose of defeating Hitler, there would remain only victors and vanquished and no international system that could provide an institutionalized structure and procedures by means of which the Western powers and the Russians could work out a solution to the power vacuum in the center of Europe. Roosevelt, then, was faced with two important and difficult postwar tasks: the need to create the beginnings of a new international system and the necessity of finding a way to prevent dangerous competition to fill the vacuum in Central Europe.

What were the various possibilities available for dealing with these tasks? One possibility was to try to recreate a new balance-of-power system. But what kind of balance-of-power system? The history of the last few centuries had seen several significantly different variants of such a system.

Roosevelt rejected the kind of balance-of-power system marked by a great deal of competition and conflict among the major powers—the kind of system that had existed during the eighteenth century that had failed to deter Napoleon from attempting to achieve hegemony and that had also failed for a number of years to form the kind of coalition needed to bring him down. In Roosevelt's view, a highly competitive balance-of-power system of this type for the postwar period would be neither desirable nor feasible. Britain would be too weak by itself to provide a military counterweight to Russia on the European continent. The United States, even with its enormous military power, would not want to or be able to bolster England for the purpose of balancing Soviet pressure in Europe. It must be remembered that Roosevelt operated on the premise—which seemed completely justified at the time— that U.S. public opinion would not tolerate leaving large U.S. military forces in Europe very long once the war ended. So the grim prospect Roosevelt had to contend with—and to avoid, if possible—was that the Soviet Union could end up dominating Europe unless the Russians could be brought into a different kind of system.

One way to avoid this dilemma, of course, would have been for the United States and Britain to forego the war objective of inflicting total defeat on Germany and Italy and to settle instead for a negotiated, compromise peace with Hitler and Mussolini. But it was most unlikely that this alternative could be made acceptable to U.S. (or British) public opinion. Besides, since the Russians too could have played this game, it would have quickly led to a race between the Western powers and the Russians to see who could first make a separate peace with Hitler in order to bring Germany in on its side of the newly emerging balance of power.

Possibly there was another way of avoiding the dangers that a power vacuum in Europe would pose. These dangers might be minimized or avoided if the Western powers and the Soviet Union got together and worked out a political division of Europe before the total defeat and occupation of Germany and Italy. But it is difficult to imagine how a political division of Europe between the Russians and the West could be successfully implemented during or immediately after the war, or be made acceptable to the U.S. people. If the thought occurred to Roosevelt, there is little indication that he regarded it as at all a feasible or desirable option. The most that could be done, and was done, was to agree on zones of occupation into which the military forces of the Soviet Union, Britain, and the United States would regroup after the defeat of Nazi Germany. This agreement on military zones of occupation reduced the immediate danger of conflict, but it was neither intended nor expected to eventuate in a political division of Europe; it was *not* part of a "spheres-of-influence" agreement at that time even though spheres of influence would emerge later on, based on the occupation zones.

There was still another possibility. If a complete division of Europe between the Western powers and the

Soviet Union was deemed impractical or undesirable, the two sides might at least agree to grant each other spheres of influence in *parts* of Europe, with Germany itself being placed under their joint military occupation. Something of the kind—a partial spheres-of-influence agreement covering Rumania, Hungary, Bulgaria, Italy, Greece, and Yugoslavia—was proposed by Churchill to Stalin at their private meeting in Moscow in October 1944 and accepted by Stalin. But Roosevelt, although initially sympathetic, felt he could not approve such an arrangement.

Roosevelt rejected the model of a highly competitive balance-of-power system, and also the idea of attempting to reduce its conflict potential by creating spheres of influence, for several reasons. First of all, he doubted—and in this he was undoubtedly right—that the U.S. public would agree to U.S. participation in such arrangements, given its historic antipathy to the European balance-of-power system. Besides, for Roosevelt to endorse or participate in a spheres-of-influence agreement would have directly contradicted the principles of self-determination and independence that he had written into the Atlantic Charter. That declaration was the major statement of Allied war aims and a major means by which Roosevelt had secured public support for an internationalist postwar foreign policy. For this reason, while Roosevelt was indeed prepared to accept predominant Soviet influence in Eastern Europe, such an outcome had to be legitimized through procedures consistent with the Atlantic Charter.

Besides, Roosevelt did not believe that a competitive balance-of-power system, even one moderated by spheres of influence in Europe, would eliminate rivalry for very long. Any such arrangements would prove to be unstable and the world would soon become divided into two armed camps—a Western democratic one and a Soviet-led one. An arms race would ensue that at best would result in a dangerous armed truce, and at worst would lead to another world war. In brief, Roosevelt foresaw the possibility that something like the cold war would emerge—that is, unless some alternative could be devised.

The only alternative, as Roosevelt saw it, was a version of the balance of power modeled on some aspects of the Concert System set up by the European powers in 1815 after defeating Napoleon. To this end Roosevelt hoped that unity and cooperation of the Allies could be maintained after the defeat of the totalitarian states. This was the option Roosevelt favored from an early stage in the war. He called it his "Great Design," and he succeeded in getting Churchill and Stalin to agree to it and to cooperate in trying to bring it about.

The Great Design called for the establishment of a postwar security system in which the United States, Great Britain, the Soviet Union—and hopefully eventually China—would form a consortium of overwhelming

power with which to keep the peace. These major powers, forming an executive committee, would consult and
cooperate with each other to meet any threat to peace,
either from the defeated powers or from any others that
might arise to threaten the peace. These four powers
would have a virtual monopoly of military power; all
other states would be prevented from having military
forces that could pose a serious threat to others. Quite
appropriately, Roosevelt called this concept the "Four
Policemen." It must be noted that such a system would
have violated the principle of sovereign equality of all
states, great or small, and hence it could not be recon-
ciled with the Atlantic Charter.

Turning now to Roosevelt's "Grand Strategy" for
achieving his Great Design, we note, first of all, that it
called for the United States, Great Britain, and the
Soviet Union to work out mutually acceptable settlements of the important territorial issues and political
problems in Europe. These settlements would be
reached through joint consultation and agreement—in
other words, through a system of collective decisionmaking, not unilateral action by either side. In this
respect Roosevelt's Great Design was influenced by the
recollection that in 1815, after the European powers
finally succeeded in defeating Napoleon, they then
formed a Concert System that relied upon frequent
meetings of foreign ministers to make joint decisions
with regard to keeping the peace, dealing with any

threats to it, and resolving any disagreements that might arise among themselves.

Instead of a balance-of-power system, therefore, Roosevelt sought to create a new Concert System that would maintain the unity and effective cooperation of the victorious Allies after the war as well. And instead of secret agreements and spheres of influence, he hoped that new governments would emerge in the occupied states of Europe through procedures and policies that were consistent with the principle of national self-determination and independence.

To this fundamental strategic concept Roosevelt added other elements: reliance on high-level personal diplomacy, confidence-building measures, and conciliation and appeasement of the Soviet Union's legitimate security needs.

As for Roosevelt's tactics, the emphasis was on the need to minimize conflict and disagreement in day-to-day relations, the importance of leaning over backward not to give offense, and the avoidance of behavior that might be interpreted by the Soviets as indicating hostility or lack of sympathy.

Particularly at the level of tactics, but to some extent also at the level of strategy, there were some alternatives to the choices Roosevelt made. Generally speaking, the choice of a design-objective—a particular Grand Design for policy—does of course constrain the choice of strategy; and the choice of a particular strategy constrains in turn the choice of tactics. One strategy may be more appropriate for pursuing a given design-objective than another, and one set of tactics may be more effective than another. These choices of strategy and tactics are likely to be influenced by the policymakers' beliefs as to the relative efficacy of alternative strategies and tactics. It is entirely possible, therefore, as experience accumulates in attempting to achieve a long-range design-objective, that policymakers will be led to question their initial choice of tactics and/or strategy but without questioning—initially at least—the correctness and legitimacy of the design-objective itself.

We have now identified Roosevelt's Grand Design, his Grand Strategy, and his Tactics. *Each of them was supported by a set of cognitive beliefs having to do with the characteristics of the Soviets.* These beliefs constituted the knowledge base on which Roosevelt could draw in attempting to gain cognitive legitimacy for his overall postwar plans from members of his administration, Congress, and the public. From available historical materials it is relatively easy to identify the various cognitive beliefs about the Soviets that supported each component of the overall policy.

How well founded were these beliefs about the Soviets on which Roosevelt's postwar policy rested? It must be recognized that the exigencies and pressures of the wartime situation—the need to get along with the Russians in order to ensure the defeat of the enemy powers—no doubt powerfully motivated Roosevelt to develop a somewhat benign, optimistic image of the Soviets. But was that image therefore naïve? Was it simply wishful thinking to believe that the Soviets might participate in a cooperative postwar system of some kind?

Roosevelt's hopes and beliefs regarding the Soviets cannot be so easily dismissed as naïve. The content of some of Roosevelt's policies and his judgment of the Soviet Union were indeed criticized by some persons at the time. But suffice it to say that the naïveté regarding the Soviet Union that Roosevelt has been charged with was much more apparent after the failure of his hopes for postwar cooperation with the Russians than before. During the war itself, while Roosevelt was alive, and even for a while thereafter, many specialists on the Soviet Union (for example, Charles Bohlen) and other foreign policy experts were not at all sure that his policy would fail. Many of the beliefs about the Soviet Union that supported Roosevelt's Grand Design enjoyed a considerable measure of plausibility and support. His policies and the beliefs that supported them were not a hasty improvisation but reflected careful deliberation on his part and on the part of quite a few advisers. Even skeptics about the Soviet Union thought there was a chance that Soviet leaders would cooperate, out of self-interest, with Roosevelt's Grand Design. The generally successful wartime cooperation with the

Soviets reinforced these hopes, and they were further strengthened by Roosevelt's assessment of Stalin's postwar intentions and the general endorsement he obtained from Stalin of the concept of a cooperative postwar security system.

It should be noted, further, that despite his generally optimistic personality and outlook, Roosevelt did not hide from himself or others close to him the possibility that his image of the Soviets might be defective and that his hopes for postwar cooperation might eventually prove unfounded. He realized, in other words, that he was taking a calculated risk, and he remained sensitive to any Soviet actions that threatened the success of his postwar plans or appeared to call into question the validity of the premises on which it was based. Roosevelt was also ready to undertake remedial measures to bring Stalin back into line whenever necessary.

## Domestic Constraints Affecting the Implementation of Roosevelt's Postwar Policies

In addition to the constraints already noted on Roosevelt's choice of a "realist"-oriented postwar security system, domestic pressures hampered his effort to secure and maintain strong legitimacy for his policy. Although he strongly favored the Four Policemen concept, Roosevelt was most cautious in publicizing it. He did not seriously attempt to inform and educate public opinion on the matter because he feared that such an effort would shatter the domestic consensus for an internationalist postwar foreign policy. Roosevelt felt he had to blur the difference between his realistic approach to power and security, and the Wilsonian idealists' desire for a system of collective security based on the creation of another, stronger League of Nations. Roosevelt did speak about his Four Policemen concept privately with a number of influential opinion leaders. But when he attempted to float a trial balloon to publicize the idea in an interview with a journalist, it triggered a sharply negative reaction at home from the idealists. As a result, Roosevelt backed away from further efforts to educate public opinion in order to gain understanding and legitimacy for his Four Policemen concept.

From an early stage in World War II Roosevelt had strongly opposed setting up a new League of Nations after the war. He felt that the task of enforcing the peace would have to be left to the Four Policemen for a number of years. However, once again to avoid political troubles at home, Roosevelt bowed to the pressure of the idealists, who wanted the United Nations set up before the war was over. Roosevelt therefore acquiesced when Secretary of State Cordell Hull, who himself was closely identified with the Wilsonian idealists, gradually transformed the Four Policemen idea into what became the Security Council of the United Nations. Roosevelt consoled himself with the thought that it was not the early establishment of the United Nations and the format of the Security Council that were critical but, rather, that the United States and the Soviet Union should preserve a friendly and cooperative relationship, and that they should settle all important issues between them outside the Security Council and work together to maintain peace.

Roosevelt, as suggested earlier, could not approve an old-fashioned spheres-of-influence arrangement in Europe. He feared that it would be perceived by the U.S. public as another example of how the cynical, immoral European powers periodically got together to make secret agreements to divide up the spoils at the expense of weaker states, and hence as a violation of the principle of national self-determination and independence. Such a development in public opinion, Roosevelt foresaw, could jeopardize his postwar plans right from the beginning. But at the same time Roosevelt recognized that the Soviet Union's legitimate security needs in Eastern Europe would have to be satisfied. Since the Red Army was occupying Eastern Europe and would likely move into Central Europe as well, the Soviet Union could do as it wished there in any case. The United States would not employ force or threats of force to prevent or to dissuade the Soviets from creating friendly regimes and making territorial changes in Eastern Europe. This was understood and accepted even by those of Roosevelt's advisers—including Soviet experts in the State Department—who were most negative in their view of Soviet communism.[4]

From the standpoint of maintaining the U.S. public's support for his postwar policy it was terribly important for Roosevelt, first, that the Soviet Union should define its security needs in Eastern Europe in *minimal* terms and, second, that it should go about securing friendly regimes in Eastern Europe in ways that the United States and Britain could agree to and that would not flagrantly conflict with the principles of the Atlantic Charter. What was at stake for Roosevelt was the legitimacy in the eyes of the U.S. public of his entire plan for a postwar security system based on cooperation with the Soviet Union. If Soviet behavior in Eastern Europe were seen by the U.S. public as flagrantly conflicting with the principle of national self-determination and independence, it would create the image of an expansionist Soviet Union—one that could not be trusted.

Roosevelt hoped—perhaps somewhat naïvely—that the potential conflict between the Soviet Union's security requirements and the principles of the Atlantic Charter could be avoided or minimized in a number of ways. During the war he attempted to persuade Stalin that the complete defeat and disarming of Germany and the arrangements being made to weaken and control postwar Germany would do more to guarantee Soviet security than would Soviet territorial gains and the imposition of tight-fisted Soviet control over Eastern Europe.

Roosevelt also attempted to get Stalin to understand the difficulties with U.S. public opinion that would be created should the Soviet Union fail to cooperate in working out territorial settlements and political arrangements in Eastern Europe that did not flagrantly conflict with the commitment to uphold the principle of national self-determination and independence. In effect, Roosevelt was pleading for Stalin to show self-restraint; he hoped that Stalin would cooperate at least to the extent of providing a "cosmetic" façade to the creation of pro-Soviet regimes in Poland and other Eastern European countries. Stalin in fact seemed disposed to cooperate. Cosmetic solutions were in fact patched up several times. Thus Roosevelt and most of his advisers thought they had achieved that goal at the Yalta Conference in early 1945. But their optimism was quickly shaken by new difficulties with the Russians over interpretation of the Yalta agreements regarding Poland. Within a few months of becoming president, Truman, too, succeeded in patching up the disagreement over Poland; but once the war was over, distrust of Soviet intentions mounted in Congress and among the public. People increasingly interpreted Soviet behavior in Eastern Europe as a harbinger of more ambitious expansionist aims, and it became more difficult to arrest the drift into the cold war.

Roosevelt died before these developments made themselves felt so acutely as to force major changes in his policy toward the Soviet Union. Among the many disadvantages Truman labored under in his effort to make a success of Roosevelt's policy was the reassertion by Congress, once the war ended in the summer of 1945, of its role in foreign policy. Truman was genuinely committed to trying to achieve Roosevelt's Great Design—that is, as best he could, given the fact that Roosevelt never took Truman into his confidence and also given the fact that Roosevelt's advisers had various opinions as to how best to deal with the Russians.

Pressures and circumstances of this kind hampered Truman's ability to continue efforts to make Roosevelt's policy succeed, though he certainly tried to do so for a while; eventually, however, Truman was led to move step by step away from that policy to the policy of containment and balance of power associated with the cold war. But only gradually and, it should be noted, with considerable reluctance did Truman replace the image of the Soviets that supported Roosevelt's postwar policy with the quite different set of beliefs about the Soviet Union associated with the cold war.

Several hypotheses help to explain why the transition to containment and cold war was slow and difficult. First, as already noted, the exigencies and situational pressures of the wartime situation provided strong—indeed, compelling—incentives for giving credence to evidence that supported the benign, optimistic image of the Soviets. And the generally successful wartime collaboration with the Soviets reinforced hopes that this image was sound and would prove to be stable. But to recognize this fact is by no means to imply that Roosevelt and, later, Truman were engaged in biased information processing of incoming data on Soviet behavior in order to confirm an existing optimistic image of the Russians. Rather, the record shows that incoming information on new Soviet actions was interpreted sometimes as undermining some of the optimistic beliefs on which Roosevelt's policy rested but at other times as reinforcing them, so that there were ups and downs rather than a straight-line, steady erosion of the optimistic image of the Soviets.

A second hypothesis helping to account for the gradualness of the transition to the cold war is to be found in the very nature of policy legitimacy. Once a foreign policy is established and achieves a degree of policy legitimacy—both normative and cognitive legitimacy—in the eyes of top policymakers themselves and enough other influential political actors, it is difficult for policymakers to contemplate replacing that policy with one that is radically different. An entirely new foreign policy will require new normative and/or cognitive legitimation. The uncertainty and expected difficulty of achieving adequate legitimation for a different policy reduces incentives for engaging in policy innovation and strengthens incentives to "save" the existing policy if only via modifications at the margins. *Substantial* erosion in public support for the existing policy and/or effective political pressure by influential critics would appear to be a necessary condition for overcoming the momentum of an established policy and for motivating top policymakers to address seriously the need for a basic overhauling of existing policy.

What this suggests, more specifically in the case at hand, is that disavowal of Roosevelt's policy of cooperation with the Soviet Union carried with it the risk of undermining the basic legitimation of any internationalist foreign policy, thereby encouraging a return to isolationism. The two alternative "realist" internationalist foreign policies that Roosevelt had rejected had, as noted earlier, severe disadvantages with regard to public acceptability. In the end Truman rejected both the spheres-of-influence and balance-of-power alternatives, choosing instead a somewhat vaguely defined "containment" strategy, which he coupled with support for the United Nations. (That the containment strategy and the ensuing cold war could take on some of the characteristics of a balance-of-power system—though bipolar rather than multipolar as in the eighteenth and nineteenth centuries—and eventually lead to a de facto spheres-of-influence arrangement was not clearly foreseen.)

The transition from Roosevelt's policy to containment and the cold war was, as noted earlier, a gradual one. Its relationship to the architecture of Roosevelt's policy is of particular interest: the change started at the level of tactics, worked upward to strategy, and finally extended to the level of design-objectives.

Dissatisfaction with the way in which Roosevelt's policy was working emerged quite early, and it focused initially and for some time on the *tactics* that were being employed. The "kid gloves" treatment of the Russians was rejected as counterproductive by some advisers and officials, among them Averell Harriman, who was to become particularly influential with Truman's administration. It is true that Truman, quite soon after replacing Roosevelt, adopted a "get tough" approach to the Russians. But as John Gaddis and others have noted, "getting tough" was initially meant to apply only to a change in tactics in dealing with the Russians. This tactical innovation was to remain for some months part of an effort intended not so much to change Roosevelt's Great Design and his strategy but to achieve them more effectively.[5]

In effect, Truman *improvised* an alternative to Roosevelt's Great Design over a period of time, working as it were from the bottom up—from tactics to strategy to design-objectives—rather than deductively, as Roosevelt had done, from design-objectives to strategy to tactics.

As it evolved, the new cold war policy encountered serious difficulties in its ability to gain acceptance from the standpoint of both desirability and feasibility. In striving to attain policy legitimacy with Congress and the public for its cold war policies, the Truman administration was led into a considerable rhetorical oversimplification and exaggeration of the Soviet threat, one that rested on a new "devil image" of the Soviets and a new premise to the effect that the U.S.-Soviet conflict was a zero-sum contest. The struggle to maintain policy legitimacy for the cold war led in time to considerable rigidification in the supporting beliefs and the unwillingness of U.S. policymakers to subject them to continual testing that stands in sharp contrast to Roosevelt's and Truman's initial willingness to reassess the policy premises of the earlier policy on the basis of new information.

By way of conclusion, I offer the following list of points that have emerged from this analysis of the difficulties Roosevelt experienced in his efforts to obtain policy legitimacy for his postwar plans. First, U.S. isolationist sentiment was not powerful enough, once the United States got into the war, to prevent or hamper Roosevelt's ability to commit the country to an internationalist postwar policy. Roosevelt, however, was definitely hampered in pursuing the particular internationalist security plan that he favored by the strong idealist wing of the internationalist forces in the United States. The idealists felt that World War II provided a second chance to realize Woodrow Wilson's shattered dreams for collective security through a strong League of Nations. Roosevelt, on the other hand, believed this idealist approach to postwar security was naïve and that it would not be effective. But, in order not to jeopardize domestic support for the war and in order not to risk shattering the internationalist coalition that favored U.S. participation in some kind of postwar security system, Roosevelt shied away from trying to educate public opinion to understand and support his hard-boiled realist approach. Roosevelt felt he could not afford a direct confrontation with the Wilsonian idealists. To consolidate opinion behind U.S. war aims he issued the Atlantic Charter, which restated the country's historic idealist aspirations for national self-determination and equality of nations. And to avoid divisive controversy with the idealists, Roosevelt gradually diluted and modified his Four Policemen concept for postwar security and accepted instead the creation of the United Nations organization much earlier than he had thought desirable.

Thus, Roosevelt did secure normative legitimation for an international postwar foreign policy. But the means he employed for this purpose—the principles embodied in the Atlantic Charter—severely hampered his ability to design and pursue the particular kind of postwar security system he favored. One is struck, therefore, by the fundamental internal policy contradiction that plagued Roosevelt's efforts to put his Great Design for postwar cooperation with the Soviet Union into practice. For, in fact, the very national values and aspirations that he appealed to effectively to secure normative legitimation for an internationalist foreign policy served at the same time to impose severe constraints on the strategic flexibility he needed in order to deal with Eastern European issues.

Roosevelt's Grand Strategy called for accommodating the security needs of the Soviet Union in Eastern Europe; but the moral legitimation of his overall policy stood in the way. Roosevelt—and Truman later—found it very difficult to work out arrangements in Eastern Europe that would at the same time satisfy the Russians and not alienate idealist U.S. opinion that thought that thereby the principles of national self-determination and independence were being jeopardized. Roosevelt, and for a while Truman as well, continued to try to patch up arrangements in Eastern Europe (even "cosmetic" solutions) that would be acceptable both to Russian leaders and to U.S. idealists. Their efforts eventually failed as time ran out; the U.S. image of the Soviets hardened and Truman began to improvise an alternative policy toward the Soviets.

The lesson that emerges from this experience is that a foreign policy is vulnerable if, as in this case, the means employed to secure normative legitimation of the policy at home conflict with the requirements of the grand strategy for achieving the design-objectives of that policy.

## Public Opinion and the Problem of Evaluating Foreign Policy

Any complex long-range foreign policy such as Roosevelt's Grand Design or the Nixon-Kissinger détente policy needs considerable time to achieve its objectives. Such politics cannot be achieved overnight: one summit meeting between the heads of state will not do it; neither will one overall agreement or one decisive action. Nor can one even expect steady progress toward the long-range objective. It is more reasonable to expect occasional ups and downs.

Any long-range policy also needs to be evaluated along the way. We expect a president and his administration to engage in objective, well-informed evaluations of the policies they are pursuing. Policy evaluation of Roosevelt's approach to the Russians—and of Nixon's détente policy—involve questions such as the following: Is the long-range goal of a "cooperative" U.S.-Soviet relationship defined clearly enough—that is, does the administration have a clear enough notion of what it is striving to accomplish? Is the *general strategy* the administration is employing to achieve that long-range objective a sound one; and is the strategy working well enough, or does it need to be changed in some way? Are the day-to-day *tactics* that are being utilized to implement that strategy well conceived? Are they working, or do they need to be changed?

These questions associated with policy evaluation, it may be noted, have to do with the "cognitive legitimacy" of a policy—that is, the basis for the president's claim that he knows what he is doing; that he understands well enough the nature of the opponent and the forces at work in the world situation, and that he knows how to use the means available to him in order to achieve the long-range objective of his policy.

The evaluation of an ongoing policy is difficult to begin with, from a purely intellectual and analytical standpoint. It is all the more difficult if the monitoring and evaluation of the policy is unduly influenced by the play of domestic politics.

A president who pursues a long-range foreign policy in a democracy such as ours runs into some formidable problems. In the absence of policy legitimacy the character of U.S. politics, the role of the modern mass media in our political life, and the volatile nature of public opinion combine to subject the president's pursuit of long-range foreign policy objectives to constant scrutiny and evaluations. As a result, the president finds himself forced to defend his long-range policy on a month-to-month—if not also a day-to-day—basis. When this happens, a shortened and often distorted time perspective is introduced into the already difficult task of evaluating the policy and the related task of deciding whether changes in strategy and tactics are necessary.

One of the characteristics of the U.S. public is its impatience for quick results and its demand for frequent reassurances that a policy is succeeding. This impatience is often fed and exploited by the mass media and by political opponents of the administration's policy. These domestic political factors interfere with the ability of a president to pursue a long-range policy with the patience and persistence that is needed. The play of public opinion and politics can distort the difficult task of evaluating the policy; it can erode its legitimacy; it can force changes in that policy before it has had a chance to prove itself.

Faced with the volatile tendencies of U.S. public opinion, a president and his advisers must attempt to carefully control the public's impatience for quick results. They must also offer meaningful assurances that the cognitive premises of their policy goals and of the strategy and tactics employed on behalf of these goals are being subjected to careful, objective evaluation. They must also control their own tendency to pander to the public's demand for quick, dramatic results as a way of making up for the inadequate legitimacy that their policy enjoys. On this score, Kissinger and Nixon can be criticized for having pandered to the public's impatience for quick results and its tendency to be impressed by dramatic achievements of a symbolic rather than substantive import. In the early years of détente, Nixon and Kissinger were able to come up with spectacular events that seemed to offer assurance that détente was working—the trips to Beijing, the summits with Soviet leaders in Moscow and Washington, the multitude of agreements. But thereby Nixon and Kissinger helped to create a frame of mind and a set of expectations in the public that worked against them later on when they had no more rabbits to pull out of the hat, at least for the time being. Day-to-day "successes"—whether real successes or contrived public-relations-type successes—are not only a poor substitute for genuine policy legitimacy; they can easily end up helping to erode whatever legitimacy has been achieved for a complex, long-range policy.

## CHAPTER THREE
## STABLE PEACE AND DEMOCRATIC PEACE

Stability is perhaps the most important
word in the diplomat's dictionary. In its
name, autocrats are embraced, dictators
are coddled and tyrants are courted.

—Natan Sharansky

I thought it would be appropriate to recall the origins
of my interest in the subject of stable peace. In 1992,
when Shimon Shamir from Tel-Aviv University and I
were fellows at the United States Institute for Peace, we
discussed how best to characterize the state of peace that
had emerged in Israeli-Egyptian relations. It was clear to
both of us that some way of identifying different types
of peace was needed to replace the simple distinction
between war and peace.

Shamir's preferred typology at that time was a four-
fold distinction among "adversarial peace," "restricted

peace," "rapprochement," and "cooperative peace." Somewhat dissatisfied with this typology, I suggested as an alternative a threefold distinction among "precarious peace," "conditional peace," and "stable peace."[1]

Indeed, over time a number of other typologies have been advanced. Clearly there is a need to bring together the different concepts and terms used to distinguish types of peace, to show the considerable extent to which they overlap, and to expose various ambiguities in their definitions. If a common, shared set of concepts can be developed, it will benefit research by providing a basis for a systematic and cumulative research on this important question. It has not been entirely clear when investigators were in agreement or disagreement in applying elements of their typologies to different empirical cases.

My own typology was influenced by important writings of scholars—in particular, Karl Deutsch and Kenneth Boulding. Deutsch's concept of peace pointed in the right direction. His classic description of a "security community" emphasized that the peace it brought with it was based, among other things, on "the real assurance that the members of that community will not fight each other physically, but will settle their disputes in some other way."[2] This identifies a core element of the definition of "stable peace." Moreover, his emphasis on the importance of developing a community remains of prime importance, though whether it is either a necessary or a sufficient condition for the emergence of stable peace in all situations needs to be subjected to empirical testing. However, I found Deutsch's concept of peace somewhat ambiguous and his various definitions of it inconsistent. Boulding's concept of stable peace was quite useful but in need of clarification and additional specification. He defined peace as a situation in which the probability of war is so small that it does not enter into the calculations of any of the people involved.[3] The full research program envisaged by Deutsch and his colleagues was never completed, though several books were published after his major publication.[4]

Balanced assessments of Deutsch's seminal contribution have been provided by a number of scholars, quite recently by Emanuel Adler and Michael Barnett.[5] Perhaps the most systematic follow-up to Deutsch's book was the important study by Stephen R. Rock.[6] But I find inconsistency and some ambiguity in his treatment.

As Erik G. Yesson reminds us, all these definitions evoke Immanuel Kant's insistence in his classic work *Perpetual Peace* that peace is not simply a "suspension of hostilities" but rather "an end to all hostilities," which means the nullification of "all existing reasons for a future war."[7]

I would like to clarify my own threefold typology, which emphasizes the extent to which peace depends upon deterrent and compellent threats, as follows:

*Precarious peace* is a relationship of acute conflict between two states that may have already engaged in warfare in the past and/or have been and are on the verge of major war. At least one state is dissatisfied with the status quo, and one or both see the use of military force as legitimate for either defending or changing the status quo. Peace, therefore, means little more than the temporary absence of armed conflict. Such a peace depends for its maintenance not merely on "general deterrence," a term introduced into the literature some years ago by Patrick Morgan, but may require frequent use of "immediate deterrence"—that is, military alerts and deployments, or issuance of deterrence threats in war-threatening crises. The Arab-Israeli relationship until recent times and the Indo-Pakistani relationship over many years are examples of "precarious peace."

*Conditional peace* describes a substantially less acute, less precarious relationship. General deterrence plays the predominant role in maintaining peace except in quite infrequent crises or precrisis situations, in which one or both sides feel it necessary to resort to activities that provide immediate deterrence to avoid outbreak of war. The U.S.-Soviet relationship during the cold war qualifies as an example of "conditional peace." During that era there were occasional but infrequent diplomatic crises over Berlin, Cuba, and the Middle East in which general deterrence was supplemented with immediate deterrence. Neither in precarious peace nor in conditional peace does either side rule out initiating military force as an instrument of policy, and deterrent and compellent threats of doing so do occur.

*Stable peace* is a relationship between two states in which neither side considers employing force, or even making a threat of force, in any dispute, even serious disputes, between them. Deterrence and compellence backed by threats of military force are simply excluded as instruments of policy. Two states that enjoy stable peace may continue to have serious disputes, but they share a firm understanding that such disputes must be dealt with by nonmilitary means. For example, in the Suez crisis of 1956, President Eisenhower made strong, credible threats of economic sanctions to pressure the British to withdraw their forces from the Suez Canal area.

This typology—and indeed others—is conceptual in the first instance. As in any typology, it can only be the starting point for attempting to characterize actual relationships between states and to undertake empirical research. Types should not be reified; they should not be imposed on historical cases in a mechanical, simplistic way that obscures relevant uncertainties and complexities. The test of a typology should be whether it facilitates empirical research and development of theory. A comprehensive research program on this fundamental aspect of international relations entails a number of questions and problems that I will now address.

One of these is the task of determining whether two states—whether or not they are democracies—enjoy stable peace. This may be difficult to discern for various reasons, and it is a matter of finding ways to distinguish between the existence of conditional peace and stable peace. The continued absence of war and war-threatening crises in a relationship, however significant in and of itself, is not sufficient to establish the existence of stable peace. Peace between two states may not yet have been subjected to tough tests, such as disputes severe enough to stimulate one side or the other to consider or make use of immediate deterrence. In fact, if one sees beneath the surface of peace that the military on one or the other side is still preparing secret contingency plans of a serious kind for possible use of force, then one must question whether stable peace really exists. In such cases, general deterrence may still play a role, though not a conspicuous one, in supporting what appears to be stable peace.

Moreover, while peace appears to be stable, leaders and publics on one or both sides may feel that it is not a sufficiently cordial relationship that includes all desired forms, activities, and institutions of a cooperative nature such as confidence-building measures, cooperation on nonsecurity issues, and dispute resolution mechanisms. Thus, Israeli scholars have felt it necessary to distinguish between "cold peace" and "warm peace" to call attention to the fact that Israel and Egypt have never managed to develop the kinds of interactions with each other that include the repertoire of warm, friendly relations between neighbors. Can one say, nonetheless, that stable peace exists between Israel and Egypt? Has peace between them been subjected to tough tests? Does either side have contingency plans for possible use of force or for purposes of backing up immediate deterrence threats that become necessary in a future crisis?

One may take note of the possibility, too, that while the dominant leadership on both sides, enjoying what appears to be stable peace, believes in and acts in accord with the requirements of stable peace, important elements of the elite or counterelites and of the public in general still regard the other side as posing a latent threat to its security. When this suspicion prevails, stable peace may be vulnerable. Such a state of affairs may characterize U.S.-Soviet relations since the end of the cold war. Certainly, leaders and elements of their publics have moved from the conditional peace that characterized U.S.-Soviet relations during the cold war toward stable peace; but important elements of their political-military elite and of their publics evidently question whether general deterrence is no longer necessary and whether the possible need for resort to immediate deterrence in the future can be safely excluded.

A better example of stable peace is the relationship among most of the Western European countries embraced by the European Union and NATO, a development in the post–World War II era that engaged the interest of Karl Deutsch and his colleagues, and many others.

The research agenda should also include the study of the conditions under which and the processes by which states move from a relationship of precarious or conditional peace to one of stable peace. There may be many paths to stable peace: negotiated settlements; regime transitions (especially democratization); demographic changes; changes in military, economic, and transportation technologies; and social or normative changes. There are few studies of this kind as yet and many historical examples of such a development that should be studied and compared. A leading example, of course, is the already mentioned emergence of a security community in Western Europe. Other possible examples include Argentina and Brazil; South Africa and its neighbors after the end of apartheid; and the United States, Canada, and Mexico.

Some years ago I asked Magnus Jerneck, who was then visiting Stanford University, whether Swedish or other Scandinavian scholars had studied the transition to stable peace in the relations among Scandinavian countries. Jerneck, a political scientist at Lund University, checked with his colleagues in the history department at Lund. He was told that although the phenomenon was well known, no systematic studies of it existed.

Accordingly, Jerneck and several of his colleagues formed an interdisciplinary research team that has stimulated much research.

Obviously, the interest in stable peace—its emergence, what it is based upon, how it can be recognized, and so on—overlaps with the democratic peace thesis that has received a great deal of attention and discussion, particularly in the United States. Much of this scholarly attention has focused on efforts to explain what it is about being a democratic polity that is the basis for the absence of war between two democratic states. Not enough attention has been given to the study of *historical transitions* in the relations between democratic states that have resulted in stable peace between them. It may matter, for example, whether one state in the dyad became a democracy through civil war, international war, revolution, occupation, or gradual political development.

In fact, much of the research regarding stable peace among democratic states does not distinguish clearly between conditional peace and stable peace. Distinguishing between these two types of democratic peace would be facilitated if more attention were given to historical studies of transitions to stable peace. An exemplary study of such transitions is Stephen Rock's study of how the British employed a strategy of appeasement of the United States toward the end of the nineteenth century to remove the serious war-threatening disputes in their relations, thus paving the way from conditional to stable peace in their relationship.[8]

The earlier Deutsch study and others have traced the development of stable peace among Western European countries. These other studies have focused on deliberate efforts after World War II to create the attitudes, policies, and structures for a new peaceful relationship between France and Germany, for example.[9] Such studies are important because they indicate that certain efforts and strategies can be adopted to bring into being a relationship of stable peace. Studies are needed of many other cases of transitions to stable peace. For example, considerable research is already available on the relations of the United States with Canada and Mexico, but it should be reviewed in order to identify and explain the critical turning point that led to what seems clearly to have become stable peace.

Broad generalizations about conditions and processes that have led to stable peace in different situations may be possible, but it would be well to act on the presumption that this process, as with so many other phenomena in international relations, is subject to equifinality (referred to as "multiple causation" by some scholars). That is, similar outcomes (e.g., stable peace) can occur through different causal processes. Even when a common factor can be identified, in many cases the question remains whether that is a necessary or sufficient condition for the emergence of stable peace, and how much causal weight can be attributed to it.

What I have been suggesting is that it is best to regard the "democratic peace" phenomenon as a subset of the broader general phenomenon of stable peace. In this connection, I question whether stable peace is possible only and has occurred only between countries that are democracies. A more comprehensive research program would look for historical cases of stable peace between countries that are not democracies, or between states only one of which is a democracy. It is important to apply the distinction between conditional and stable peace also in such studies.

Finally, I believe it is important that a full research program should include efforts to judge whether lessons can be drawn from historical studies that may be of some relevance for efforts to move relations between adversarial states to stable peace or, at least, to something approximating it. Several years ago, when I was preparing a foreword to James Goodby's *Europe Undivided*, I was struck by the fact that he was addressing the desirability and feasibility of moving U.S.-Russian relations from conditional peace to stable peace.

In sum, there are ambiguities and inconsistencies in defining the concept of peace in research that addresses the possibility of stable peace or of democratic peace. In particular, it is important to clarify whether presumed instances of stable peace blur the important distinction between conditional and stable peace. These major conceptual issues need to be addressed and clarified given their important implications for scholarship and policy.

# CHAPTER FOUR
# ANALYSIS AND JUDGMENT

I believe in the fallibility of human
nature. We continually step on our best
aspirations. We're humans. Given a
chance to screw up, we will.
                              —Brent Scowcroft

I have attempted for many years to find a way for dealing with the relationship between analysis and judgment in high-level decisionmaking. First, a few observa-
tions are necessary regarding the development of this
interest and how it emerged from awareness of the
changing historical context of foreign policy analysis.

Many scholars have attempted to develop better
policy-relevant knowledge of foreign policy problems
that must be dealt with by decisionmakers. I have
joined in this effort, but I couple it with a sober view
of the extent to which even high-quality scholarly

studies and analysis can be expected to ensure high-quality foreign policy. One must not underestimate the extent to which important policies are shaped by factors other than scholarly knowledge and objective analysis. Various political considerations and psychological factors often constrain the impact that objective analysis can have on the decisions of top-level policymakers. At the very least, however, the availability of solid knowledge and objective policy analysis can reduce the detrimental impact such factors might have on decisions. I reject, as do many others, the pessimistic conclusion that policy-relevant knowledge and good policy analysis make little difference in improving the quality of many decisions.

Some students of policymaking would argue that the sole or dominant criterion of good policy should be its "analytical rationality"—that is, identifying options likely to achieve policy objectives at acceptable levels of cost and risk. Such a view, however, reflects an overintellectualized view of foreign policy. For in designing and choosing courses of action, policymakers must be concerned not solely with meeting the ideal of analytical rationality but also with several other desiderata that will be addressed here. To highlight the necessarily broader view and more complex concerns and interests that policymakers must take into account, I have coined the term "political rationality," which is juxtaposed to "analytical rationality." What kind of impact can scholarly knowledge be expected to have on political decisionmaking? My answer to this question is that often it can be expected to make only a limited but still quite essential contribution. Why is this so? Scholarly knowledge can be only an input to, not a substitute for, hopefully competent, well-informed policy analysis of a specific problem conducted within the government. Policy analysts within and around the government have the difficult task of adapting available knowledge to the particular case on hand that top-level policymakers must address and decide.

Similarly, general knowledge of generic policymaking problems, such as deterrence, coercive diplomacy, and so on, is not a substitute for, but only an aid to, the choice of policy by high-level decisionmakers. Incidentally, much the same can be said regarding the impact of the more specialized analyses produced by competent, objective policy analysts within the government. Thus, whereas scholars and policy analysts must preoccupy themselves with the task of identifying high-quality options that meet the criterion of analytical rationality, high-level decisionmakers exercise broader judgments that take account of a variety of additional considerations.

What these additional considerations are will be addressed when we turn to a discussion of what is meant by the "judgment" of policymakers. In the early days of the RAND Corporation, Charles Hitch, who organized the Economics Division there, made an observation about the role of analysis in policymaking that has intrigued me ever since. Hitch was one of the founders of modern systems analysis. However, he emphasized that the results of even the best systems analysis should be regarded as an aid to the preparation of policy decisions, not as a substitute for the "judgment" of the policymaker. Deeply convinced that scholarly analysis can make important, often indispensable contributions to policymaking, I have tried ever since to understand what is meant by "judgment" in this context.

Psychologists have written a great deal about judgment and how it can be influenced and distorted by cognitive dynamics. I am conversant also with the literature on the impact that small-group dynamics and organizational bureaucratic behavior can have on the quality of decisions. I need not attempt to summarize or comment on these important literatures except to say that I have not found in them a complete or satisfactory answer to the question of what constitutes the "judgment" of policymakers.

The first task is to conceptualize and disaggregate "judgment" in ways that will facilitate development and assessment of the role(s) it plays in decisionmaking. I have found it necessary to replace the global notion of "judgment" with seven different types of judgment, one or more of which decisionmakers exercise in choosing policies. I will list and briefly discuss these types of judgment and then provide a detailed discussion of the first one. In addressing each type of judgment, we should at least begin to address the difficult task of considering how analysis can be helpful in disciplining that type of judgment.

## Types of Judgment in Policymaking

### Trade-Off Judgments Among Analytical Quality of an Option, the Need to Obtain Support, and Use of Time and Political Resources

In fact, three related trade-offs are at issue here. The first is the trade-off between seeking to maximize the analytical quality of the policy to be chosen (i.e., which option is most likely to achieve given policy objectives at acceptable levels of cost and risk) and needing to obtain sufficient support for the policy option that is finally chosen. Another familiar, often difficult trade-off problem arises from having to decide how much time and policymaking resources to allocate to the effort to identify the best possible option. A third trade-off problem arises from having to decide how much political capital, influence resources, and time to expend in an effort to increase the level of support for the option to be chosen. Only this type of judgment will be discussed in detail in this chapter.

*Judgments of Political Side Effects
and Opportunity Costs*

Still another type of trade-off dilemma must be recognized. The criterion of analytical rationality is applied most comfortably by the policymaker when the problem in question is "bounded"—that is, when it is insulated from other policy issues that are already on the agenda or may soon emerge. But many policy issues are embedded in broader political and policy contexts. When this is so, policymakers find it necessary to consider what effect their choice on a particular policy issue will have on their overall political standing and on other parts of their overall policy program. In choosing what to do in situations of this kind, policymakers are guided not exclusively or even primarily by the dictates of analytical rationality but may be heavily influenced by their judgment of the political side effects and opportunity costs of their choices. Of course, this is not to say that a policy choice that is "best" when judged by the criterion of analytical rationality always conflicts with the decisionmaker's political interests—indeed, it may enhance them—or that the analytically best policy choice on a particular issue will necessarily entail significant opportunity costs, but simply to recognize that such trade-off dilemmas often do arise.

## Judgments of Utility and Acceptable Risk

Policy analysts provide policymakers with relevant information for attempting to calculate the utility of different options. This task is often severely complicated by the inherent uncertainties regarding so many of the factors on which decisions and choices must be based. Although policy analysts attempt to identify relevant uncertainties and possible costs and risks, policymakers often perceive other possible costs and risks and other benefits that analysts have not considered. In the final analysis, it is the policymakers who must judge what costs and risks they are willing to accept in return for payoffs to which they attach particular value. Similarly, it is the policymakers who have to decide whether to choose an option that offers the possibility of a bigger payoff but is more risky or an option that offers less of a payoff but is less risky.

## Judgments About Short-Term and Long-Term Payoffs

Many policy problems pose a possible trade-off between short- and long-term payoffs. The conventional wisdom is that policymakers generally act to avoid short-term losses or to make short-term gains in preference to pursuing strategies for avoiding long-term setbacks or for achieving long-range gains. Judgments of this kind are easier to make when policymakers are more certain of obtaining the short-term payoffs than the long-term ones. After all, the more distant future is laden with greater uncertainties than the near term. Moreover, the short-term payoffs—either gains or avoided losses—tend to be more highly valued by most political leaders. On the other hand, there may be instances when the policymaker will forgo short-term gains or accept short-term losses if they are deemed to be modest and when long-term prospects seem to be substantial. In sum, not all trade-offs between short-term and long-term payoffs are easily resolved, and in such situations the policymaker is faced with a greater challenge for exercising judgment.

### Satisfice or Optimize

Policymakers are often faced with the need to decide whether to settle for a limited payoff in a particular situation (i.e., to "satisfice") or to strive for a substantially greater one (i.e., to optimize). The literature on complex organizations emphasizes that they are generally programmed for satisficing. Political leaders, however, are able to display more variation in making such choices, and this is another type of judgment they are sometimes called on to make.

It would be useful to study the roles that general knowledge and policy analysis play, or could play, in policymakers' judgments whether to satisfice or to optimize.

## Dealing with Value Complexity

Many problems policymakers have to address are laden with competing values and interests.[1] (These include, of course, not only the national interests of the country, insofar as they can be assessed, but also the personal and political stakes of the leaders.) Standard models of rational policymaking cannot be easily employed in such instances, insofar as the multiple values embedded in the policy problem generally cannot be reduced to a single utility function that can then be used as a criterion for choosing among options.

In such cases, policymakers must exercise several kinds of judgment to deal with the value complexity. Can a policy option be invented that may at least partially satisfy each of the competing values and interests? When such political creativity is not possible or is not forthcoming, policymakers have to judge value priorities. Which values and interests engaged by the policy problem are more important? What criterion of importance should be employed? If not all the values and interests embedded in the problem can be satisfied by the policy option that is selected, can additional policy measures be identified and put into effect later to offer some degree of satisfaction for these other values and interests?

Once again, one asks how general knowledge of international affairs and policy analysis can help policymakers deal with difficult issues raised by value complexity.

### When to Decide

Finally, policymakers are often called on to decide *when* a decision should be made. Policymakers may or may not delay making decisions to give analysts more time to come up with better policy or to muster more support for their policy choice. But here we want to call attention to the fact that other considerations may influence policymakers' sense of the timing of a decision. The urgency of the problem itself, or domestic or international constraints or both, may influence the policymakers' judgment about when to decide on a policy, quite independently of the quality of analysis available.

## Trade-Offs Among Analytical Quality, Support, and Use of Time and Political Resources in Decisionmaking

As noted, only the first category of judgments will be discussed. Academic specialists can easily fall into the error of thinking about the quality of policy decisions in too narrow a framework. Decisionmakers have to deal with the tension that often exists between policy quality and the need to choose one policy that commands enough support. Very often a measure of quality has to be sacrificed in favor of a decision that will get the kind of political support within and outside the administration that is necessary if the policy is to have a chance of being sustained.

Another trade-off in political policymaking is the one between the quality of the decision and the policymaker's sensible use of time and of political resources. A policymaker who spends a tremendous amount of time trying to arrive at a policy decision of superior quality may incur considerable costs; time is not free. Moreover, if policymakers tie up all the resources at their disposal to achieve a higher-quality decision, the analysis of other policy issues may be neglected or short-changed. (This trade-off is said to have been a problem with Henry Kissinger's style when he dominated foreign policymaking in the Nixon administration.) Policymakers also face the practical question of deciding how much of the political capital and resources at their disposal they should expend to gain support for a quality decision. They may decide to adopt a lesser policy option for which potential support is more easily gained.

These three closely related trade-off judgments are depicted in the following figure. Dealing with them requires policymakers to exercise ad hoc judgments,

**Trade-off Dilemmas in Policymaking**

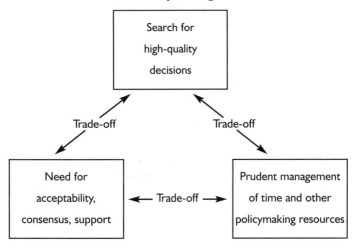

since well-defined rules for doing so are lacking. When such dilemmas arise, how, if at all, can policy-relevant theories and generic knowledge about the type of foreign policy issue in question assist in exercising judgment? This question is all the more difficult to answer because theory and generic knowledge are most directly relevant in the search for policy options of high analytical quality. This is also the focus and objective of prescriptive models of "rational" policymaking, which pay little, if any, attention to the trade-off dilemmas identified here. In fact, I know of no theory or model of decisionmaking that tells policymakers how best to manage trade-offs among quality, consensus, and management of time and policymaking resources. What is needed and lacking is what may be called a broader theory of *effective* decisionmaking that would subsume, in some way, models of analytically rational decisionmaking.

Nonetheless, several ideas can be put forward regarding the relevance of theory and general knowledge for dealing with some trade-off problems. Knowledge can be developed about strategies such as deterrence, coercive diplomacy, and crisis management; for example, distinctions can be made between strong and weak variants of these strategies, and between conditions that favor success and conditions that are likely to hamper success. Knowledge of this kind should be helpful in deciding whether a trade-off of policy quality for enhanced support would be acceptable or whether it would jeopardize the success of the weaker variant of the strategy chosen in order to gain additional support. Of course, the need for support may sometimes push the policymaker in the other direction— toward adopting a stronger variant of a strategy when a milder one would be more appropriate.

There is another way that theory and general knowledge can contribute to a better understanding of the costs and risks of trade-offs between quality and consensus. As is well known, bargaining often takes place among advocates of different policy options, and at times the dynamics of bargaining weaken the role of objective analysis during the course of a search for an option that different members of the policymaking group can agree on. However, good analysis of a policy problem can equip policymakers to anticipate what kinds and degrees of effectiveness a high-quality option is likely to lose if trade-offs are made during the bargaining in order to gain broader support. In this view, *analysis is not a substitute for bargaining but serves to inform and discipline the bargaining process* in a way that helps prevent ending up with a badly compromised policy that is likely to prove ineffectual.

Perhaps this brief discussion of basic trade-off judgments policymakers often (though not always) must make suffices to provide a richer framework, albeit a more complicated one, for considering the extent to which general knowledge of foreign policy problems and policy analysis within government can contribute to the decisions of policymakers. Quite obviously, scholarly knowledge and policy analysis can contribute more to some of the judgments policymakers make than to others. Certainly, some types of judgments—particularly when strong values are at stake—are relatively insensitive to available knowledge. In other words, there can be no assurance that even a well-developed knowledge base and competent policy analysis will have an impact when policymakers are impelled to make judgments in reaction to other considerations. Whereas scholars and policy analysts can and should concern themselves with

identifying a high-quality policy option, top policymakers have to deal with the difficult trade-off between
doing what they can to enhance the quality of a policy
and obtaining sufficient consensus and support for the
option they eventually choose. Also, top policymakers
have to decide how much time and how much of the
limited pool of resources to allocate to each of these
efforts.

In other words, a distinction can be made between
*effective* and *rational* decisionmaking. Decisionmaking is
effective when the policymaker deals reasonably well
with trade-offs between quality, support, and time and
other resources. Rational decisionmaking, on the other
hand, reflects the scholar's and the policy analyst's effort
to come up with a high-quality policy without reference to these trade-offs or to various political considerations with which the policymaker must deal.
Although scholars have provided a number of models
of rational decisionmaking, I know of no theory of
"effective" decisionmaking that seeks to improve the ad
hoc judgments top policymakers often feel obliged to
make.

This remains an important problem that requires
additional research and reflection. A few suggestions are
offered here to stimulate efforts to link analysis more
closely to judgments that decisionmakers are compelled
to make.

## Suggestions for Additional Research and Reflection

Cognitive psychologists have produced an impressive body of experimental research on various attribution errors and biases, but they do not seem to have given much attention to the types of judgmental problems discussed here. It surely will not tax their ingenuity and research methods to devise useful studies of this kind. Several suggestions are offered here as possibly useful starting points. First, as noted at the outset of the chapter, it will be necessary to disaggregate the global concept of "judgment" and develop a typology of different kinds of judgment that often enter into high-level decisionmaking.

Second, it will be necessary to treat the level of support thought to be necessary or desirable by a policymaker as a variable, one that will be sensitive to the *type of policy* being addressed and to the situational context. For example, in making decisions in diplomatic crises that carry large risks, policymakers may feel it necessary to give greater weight to choosing a high-quality option rather than one of lower quality that will gain more support. For other types of problems, the trade-off may be weighted in favor of gaining more solid support. Moreover, the concept of "support" in a democracy such as ours itself needs to be disaggregated: *Whose* support is particularly needed by a president for different types of policies in different situations? Also, the *amount* of support judged to be necessary or at least desirable can vary for different policies and in different situations. Not to be overlooked is that in some foreign policy situations, presidents can muster more support *after* they act decisively—that is, the well-known "rally-around-the-flag" phenomenon. On the other hand, they must also be sensitive to the possibility that initial support may decline over a period of time if the policy chosen runs into difficulties and mounting costs.

A third factor that future research on questions of judgment may want to take into account is personality variables that probably affect how different individuals diagnose and deal with trade-off problems.

Experimental-type research on these questions can probably be usefully abetted by interviews with executives who have accumulated a great deal of experience in exercising various types of judgment. Do such persons operate with implicit or explicit criteria, rules of thumb, maxims, guidelines in making different types of judgment? Do they believe that they learn better judgment primarily through personal experience or also from the experience of others? Notwithstanding the limitations of self-reports in research of this kind, interviews of executives (and participant-observers of executive decisionmaking) may yield useful hypotheses for additional examination.

One possible research design: Request executives to identify (1) an instance of what they consider to have been an example of their exercise of good judgment and (2) another example of what they consider to have been bad judgment. The interviewer might probe to have the executives describe their understanding of the trade-off faced, what it consisted of, how the trade-off was analyzed and evaluated with the benefit of what kind of information and advice, and why they dealt with it in the way described.

I will turn now to the question of how one might introduce the judgmental aspect of decisionmaking into education curricula. One possibility: Public policy schools and business schools might generate case studies that report how experienced executives have tried to deal with different types of judgmental problems by making use of available policy analysis or working in the absence of such analytical studies. Such case studies might be drawn from research based on interviews with executives to which reference has already been made.

The objective of having students read and discuss these case studies would be to sensitize them to the complexity and different types of judgment that executives are called upon to make and, whenever possible, to call attention to the role that analytical studies of the problem played or might have played. A related question: What kinds of factual information would have been relevant and of some use?

Another pedagogical technique might make use of well-designed simulations. A variety of decisional problems that pose trade-off dilemmas could be developed. Students would be asked questions about each case, designed to bring out their understanding of the nature of the trade-off dilemma, their identification of different ways in which it might be dealt with, their judgment as to how best to deal with it, and why. After each student completed the exercise, classroom discussion would follow, and an effort would be made to reach some consensus as to these questions or at least to identify the major preferred solutions. At the end of a series of such exercises, students would be asked to address the question of whether guidelines for assisting judgment could be formulated and how they might be used. As a follow-up, experienced executives might be asked to evaluate the students' guidelines and, perhaps, some of the judgments expressed in the simulated cases.

In concluding, I call attention to the need for studies of the other six types of judgment identified earlier in the chapter.

## CHAPTER FIVE
## THE ROLE OF COUNTERFACTUALS
## IN "MISSED OPPORTUNITIES"

During the 1990s, the Clinton administration did too little to shape the world;
more recently, the administration of
George W. Bush has often tried to do
too many things in the wrong way. The
result, though, is the same: We risk
squandering the historic opportunity at
hand.
—Richard N. Haass

I begin this chapter by noting that counterfactual
analysis and "mental experiments"—another term for
counterfactual analysis—have a long and often distinguished history.[1] This chapter focuses on a loose use of
counterfactual analysis that is often employed in refer-
ring to "missed opportunities" in history that would have
yielded better outcomes. Recently scholars have begun

to assess the possibility of "missed opportunities" in a more rigorous way, identifying standards and criteria that should be met before a desired outcome should qualify as a genuine "missed opportunity."[2]

Drawing on this recent literature, I begin with a general summary of difficulties encountered in efforts to make use of counterfactual analysis in research.

First, since a counterfactual necessarily builds upon an existing case, it will be difficult to invent an acceptable counterfactual *unless* the investigator has already constructed a quite plausible explanation for the existing case. This step is important because the counterfactual varies what are thought to be the critical variables that presumably accounted for the historical outcome. If the investigator has an erroneous or questionable explanation for the historical case, then the counterfactual analysis is likely to be flawed. Similarly, if the generalization underlying the historical explanation is a probabilistic one, certain factors varied in the counterfactual exercise may have made the event less probable, but it might have occurred anyway in the absence of those particular factors.

Second, the relationship among variables hypothesized in the counterfactual case must also be supported by plausible reasoning.

Third, when many variables are part of a historical explanation (as is often the case), it will be difficult to formulate a counterfactual that includes variation of all the causal variables. Loose efforts at counterfactual analysis often ignore the complexity of explanation for the historical case.

Fourth, a historical explanation does not necessarily imply a counterfactual argument that the event would not have happened if one or another of the causal variables in the historical case had been different. There could be causal substitution; that is, other causes in the historical case might substitute for the variable in question and cause the same outcome.

Fifth, the independent variable in the historical case that is varied must be autonomous; that is, it must be separable from other independent variables that have operated to produce the outcome in the historical case. When several independent variables are interconnected so that conjunctural causation exists, as is often the case for problems that engage the interest of social scientists, it becomes difficult to invent a usable counterfactual by altering only one variable, and the complexity of the interconnected variables may be difficult to identify reliably.

Sixth, and particularly important in this chapter, if the explanation for the historical case consists of a series of events in sequence over time—that is, chains of causation involving path dependency—rather than a single, simple circumscribed event, then constructing an acceptable counterfactual becomes much more difficult. For this would require a complex counterfactual that involves a long chain of causation involving many variables and conditions. Conversely, of course, a counterfactual is easier to construct if only one or a few decisive points in a historical case determined the outcome. Short-term simple causation is generally easier to address with a counterfactual than more complex causation that involves a longer-term process.

In sum, it is not surprising that investigators should differ in their judgment of the utility of counterfactuals for explanation and theory development. Not all investigators believe that these problems are so intractable as to warrant abandoning any use of counterfactual analysis. Nonetheless, efforts to make use of counterfactuals often fail to achieve its strict requirements. This limitation is often noted by investigators, but some proceed nonetheless to do the best they can with use of counterfactuals.

As the sixth of these criteria suggests, it is very difficult to conduct a plausible, useful counterfactual analysis *when the explanation for the historical event in question is very complex.* "Complexity" can take different forms, several of which can be identified:

- *When many variables,* thought to be independent of each other, are really part of a more complex historical explanation (as is often the case), it is difficult to formulate a plausible counterfactual.
- When the historical explanation consists of *a sequential development over time,* and not a single

variable or cluster of variables at a given point in time—that is, when the explanation is not derived from a simple "before-after" comparison—then it is very difficult to formulate a plausible counterfactual case.

- When the causal variables in the historical explanation are not independent of each other but are interdependent, then formulation of a plausible counterfactual case is exceedingly difficult, since it requires identifying the many causal variables and varying them, encountering thereby the difficulty of weighing the precise weight of each variable.

We turn now to the focus of the present chapter: problems encountered in efforts to construct plausible instances of "missed opportunities." This task requires the investigator to ask whether an outcome other than the historical outcome would have been possible or likely if its causes could have been different. This question is often raised when observers are dissatisfied with a given historical outcome and argue that policymakers could have achieved a better one if they had acted differently.

Be it noted that for this exercise a robust counterfactual is required—one that purports to identify the critical variable(s) in the historical case and alternatives to it actually available (whether considered or not) that would have produced a better outcome. This type of reasoning is required to support the assertion that in a given situation there was indeed a "missed opportunity" to accomplish a better outcome.

We now consider the analysis required to support an authentic case of a missed opportunity. The historical example chosen for discussion is Woodrow Wilson's failure to compromise in order to achieve Senate ratification of the League of Nations. The failure-to-compromise explanation makes use of a very simple counterfactual: Wilson would have made the necessary compromise with Senate opponents had he not suffered a massive stroke during the course of the battle with Senate opponents. Clearly conveyed in this claim of a missed opportunity, it should be noted, is the judgment that he *should* have compromised and it was only the consequence of his stroke that prevented him from doing so. The plausibility that this was a "missed opportunity" is enhanced since two-thirds of the Senators, required for entry into the League, did indeed favor it but never had an opportunity to translate this into approval of the League.

The critical role played by the stroke in this simple counterfactual serves to relieve Wilson of political responsibility for failure of the Senate to approve U.S. adherence to the League. The stroke hypothesis has appealed to supporters of the League who strongly favored U.S. entry into the League and deplored Wilson's stubborn refusal to compromise.

This simple counterfactual, however, encounters many legitimate questions. In the first place, it over-looks the fact that Wilson's opposition to any compro-mise that would have ensured U.S. entry into the League existed well *before his stroke*. Even before the stroke, Wilson repeatedly insisted that the Senate should pass *his* version of the resolution approving U.S. partic-ipation and strongly and consistently opposed efforts made to develop a version that would achieve the required two-thirds majority. As a result, those Senators who favored entrance into the League—the "mild reservationists"—never had an opportunity to vote for a variant of Wilson's version that would achieve a two-thirds majority vote in favor. Historians and others who have analyzed this issue agree that it was Wilson's stub-born insistence that the Senate—and the Democratic Senators—should approve only his proposal for adher-ence to the League that resulted in its defeat. Many Senators and others, indeed at the time and since, have questioned the significance of the difference between Wilson's version and the available alternatives.

Wilson himself, before he became locked in the ruinous battle with the Senate, had written clearly and persuasively on the need for a president to avoid such struggles with Congress. What is a president to do when he finds himself in an impasse with Congress? Wilson had pondered this deeply. He wrote in *Constitutional Government in the United States* (1908, pp. 139–140) that if blocked by the Senate a president does not have recourse to an appeal to the nation, a tactic he might resort to when blocked by the House. "The Senate is not so immediately sensitive to opinion and is apt to grow, if anything, more stiff if pressure of that kind is brought to bear on it."

What, then, should the president do to prevent an impasse with the Senate from arising in the first place? Wilson answered this as follows: "He may himself be less stiff and offish, may himself act with the true spirit of the Constitution and establish intimate relations of confidence with the Senate on his own initiative, and not carry his plans to completion and then laying them in final form before the Senate to be accepted, or rejected, but keeping himself in confidential communication with the leaders of the Senate while his plans are in course . . . in order that there may be veritable counsel and a real accommodation of views instead of a final challenge and contest."

In his battle with the Senate over ratification of the League, however, *well before his stroke* Wilson did exactly the opposite of the sound position he articulated in his book. Indeed, Wilson showed no interest at all in dealing with the Senate in the way he had prescribed as necessary to avoid ruinous deadlocks. Recall, too, that as numerous historians have observed, at no time during the critical weeks while he was still resisting U.S. intervention in the European war was Wilson willing to

accept the argument that war against Germany was justified on idealistic grounds or for reasons of protecting
American security. Nonetheless, when war was finally
forced upon him, Wilson placed his action on the highest idealistic grounds. Indeed, Wilson was constituted
such that he could overcome the stubborn doubts he
had so conscientiously struggled with only by replacing
them with an unquestioned faith in the righteousness of
America's cause. This pattern of decisionmaking—
replacing extreme uncertainty with extreme certainty—
was characteristic of the man. Wilson could commit his
leadership and his policy to war only by embracing far-
reaching idealistic objectives. It must be a war to make
the world safe for democracy, a war to end war, a cru-
sade to usher in a new world order.

Wilson became possessed of the idea that it was his
God-given mission to ameliorate war-ravaged mankind
by so reordering the relations of the nations of the
world to avoid war in the future. By the war's end he
had fastened upon the most important item in his program, that prescribing the formulation of a League of
Nations as the very keystone. The wish to bring such an
organization into existence suffused all his thinking and
functioning.

Historians who have examined Wilson's struggle to
bring about a proper peace settlement and the League
of Nations have been struck by the series of his inexpe-
dient actions well before the final showdown with the

Senate. When the president's numerous errors in peace-making are examined in their entirety, a common thread links them. One is forced to acknowledge, as many historians have, that temperamental defects contributed to his tragic failure. One must address his complicated personal involvement in pursuing supreme goals of this character. On important occasions, Wilson was irresistibly impelled to define and structure situations confronting him in ways that excluded the very course of action that would have best served his objectives.

Once war was thrust upon him, Wilson identified himself completely with the mission of becoming the chief architect of a new world order. To this compelling motivation were wedded more basic needs. He had always wanted—needed—to do immortal work. The greatness of the noble cause he embraced provided him with justification needed for imposing his moral purpose on others who stood, as he saw it, in the way.

Organizing a League of Nations was for Wilson a particularly appealing task. As a boy and as a young man, he had joined club after club and left in its trail constitutions he revised in which he could excel as orator. Even before the war ended, certain Senators had begun to challenge his conception of a peace settlement, focusing particularly on Wilson's proposed League of Nations. This type of challenge to his authority in a sphere of political activity laden with deep personal significance set into motion an involuntary defense mechanism, which doomed Wilson to a course of defiant insistence that his will should prevail. The more critics found fault with the League, the more determined Wilson became that the League must lie at the very heart of the peace settlement.

On November 11, 1918, the day the armistice went into effect, Wilson decided to participate in the peace negotiation himself and assumed he would be selected to preside over the peace conference. Wilson's decision to do so further irritated already hostile Senators. What right did Wilson have to go to Europe as representative of the American people since he had just been personally repudiated at the polls in 1918—*personally* repudiated because he had attempted to influence the Congressional by-elections by asking the public for the equivalent of a vote of confidence? The public reaction to Wilson's announcement that he would attend the peace conference was largely negative. And a storm of criticism broke loose a few days later when he made public the names of those he had selected to serve with him as delegates to the conference. Of those Wilson named (Secretary of State Robert Lansing, Colonel Edward M. House, General Tasker H. Bliss) only one was a Republican, Henry White, a career diplomat retired from public life for almost a decade. Wilson passed over such prominent Republicans as ex-President William Howard Taft, ex-Secretary of State Elihu Root, ex-Supreme Court Justice Charles Evans

Hughes, and Dr. Charles Eliot, president of Harvard. Wilson also ignored the possibility of naming one or more Senators to the Commission or of inviting them along to the peace conference in some other capacity.

Has Wilson been unjustly accused on this occasion as well as in his subsequent blunders in dealing with the Republican-dominated Senate? The fact is that it was clear to many of his contemporaries and supporters that he was erring. His contemporaries watched in fascinated horror as, by his own actions, Wilson fired salvo after salvo at potential Republican supporters, some of whom (Taft, for example) magnanimously tried repeatedly to provide Wilson with opportunities to undo the damage he had wrought. Indeed, Wilson's blindness was a shortcoming peculiar to him. It is hard to escape the conclusion that it was Wilson's purpose throughout to eliminate the Senate from its legitimate participation in the treaty-making procedure. Wilson deliberately withheld information from the Senate on developments in the peace conference. He acted on the firm belief that he must not defer to the Senate. It must defer to him.

From the moment Wilson adopted the League as part of his peace program he became extremely possessive of it. Many others, well before Wilson did so, had sponsored and worked for the creation of such an organization. The League to Enforce Peace, for example, had raised a powerful voice on behalf of the very thing Wilson was eventually to take to heart. Yet Wilson frowned upon many of its activities. "Butters-in" and "wool gatherers" he once called its leaders. He was contemptuous of their plans for a League—plans drawn up by men of the stature of ex-President Taft. In his eagerness to retain personal control of the League project, Wilson could see all the disadvantages but none of the possible benefits of collaborating with interested elements of the public in developing support for a League. When Wilson finally engaged Colonel House to draft a version of the League, a fact that stands out, writes Ray Stannard Baker, is that "practically nothing—not a single idea—in the Covenant of the League was original with the President. His relation to it was mainly that of editor or compiler."[3]

A number of Wilson's biographers have noted that Wilson's defeat in the fight for the League fits into a pattern of behavior he had displayed earlier in public life. Professor Arthur Link, a leading Wilson historian, undertook in an early book a painstaking analysis of the bitter and unsuccessful struggle Wilson waged over the location of a graduate college against his opponents at Princeton. Link was led to remark that "a practical observer, had he studied carefully Wilson's career as president of Princeton University, might have forecast accurately the shape of things to come during the period when Wilson was president of the United States." Calling the former a microcosm of the latter, Link ascribed to Wilson's uncompromising battles both in the graduate college controversy at Princeton and in the League of Nations battle with the Senate "the character and proportions of a Greek tragedy."[4]

As president of Princeton, governor of New Jersey, and president of the United States, Wilson gained impressive early success only to encounter equally impressive political deadlocks or setbacks later on. He entered each of these offices at a time when reform was the order of the day, and with a substantial fund of goodwill to draw upon. In each position, there was an initial period during which the type of strong leadership he exercised partly in response to his inner needs coincided sufficiently with the type of leadership the external situation required for impressive accomplishments. He drove the faculty and trustees at Princeton initially to accomplish an unprecedented series of reforms. The New Jersey legislature of 1911 was a triumph of productivity in his hands. Later, he exacted a brilliant performance from the Sixty-Third Congress of the United States.

We recognize, therefore, that Wilson's personal involvement contributed importantly to the measure of his substantial political accomplishments. In each position, however, his ambition and at times imperious methods helped to generate the type of bitter opposition that blocked further successes and threatened him with serious defeats. Wilson was skillful in the tactics of leadership only so long as it was possible to get exactly what he wanted from the Princeton trustees or the legislature. He could be adept and inventive in finding ways of mobilizing political support. In the "honeymoon" period of his incumbency he could be extremely cordial, if firm; gracious, if determined; and generally willing at least to go through the motions of consulting and granting deference to those whose support he needed. It is important to note, however, that Wilson's skillfulness in these situations always rested somewhat insecurely upon the expectation that he would be able to push through his proposed legislation in essentially unadulterated form. As Wilson put it, he was willing to accept alterations of "detail" but not of the "principles" of his proposals.

Such an interpretation, taken alone, may seem highly speculative. The reader may find it more plausible in the context of Wilson's personal development, which has been analyzed and utilized in great detail for the purpose of studying Wilson's entire development and career. Briefly paraphrased here, the interpretation offered is that political leadership was the sphere of competence Wilson, as an adolescent, carved out for himself in order to derive therefrom compensation for the damaged self-esteem branded into his spirit as a child. It was particularly when performing in his favored role as interpreter and instrument of the moral aspirations of people that he considered himself to be uniquely endowed and virtually infallible. His personal needs were such that within the sphere of competence he developed he had to function "independently" and without "interference."

Wilson's need for great achievement was no doubt reinforced by the emphasis in his religion upon "good works" and "service." Early in his career Wilson developed the highly constructive strategy of committing his desire to accomplish great achievements only to reform projects that already enjoyed considerable support and were within reasonable possibility of achievement. By doing so, he committed his vast energies and leadership skills to political objectives that were both desirable and feasible.

This strategy was constructive insofar as it reduced the likelihood that, when fastened to his need for great achievements, it would encounter political opposition that would rouse anxieties and lead him into stubborn, self-defeating behavior. As noted, Wilson entered each of his executive positions at a time when reform was the order of the day, and with a substantial fund of goodwill to draw upon. The Princeton Board of Trustees, the New Jersey State Legislature, and the U.S. Congress under Democratic Party control were in each case willing to follow his call for reforms. In each position, as also noted, Wilson was initially highly successful in driving through a series of reform measures, only to encounter equally impressive deadlocks or setbacks later on.

In the last analysis, therefore, the constructive strategy proved unavailing. Wilson's leadership embodied insatiable ambition. He was unable to derive normal gratification and pleasure from his impressive achievements. ("I am so constituted that, for some reason or other, I never have a sense of triumph," he once stated.) Success in reform projects never long satisfied him. No sooner did Wilson put through one reform than he would discover another great work calling for his attention. He pressed the new reform as something urgently and immediately to be accepted.

Wilson's ambition, in other words, was compulsive. As a result, he found it difficult to pace new reform projects prudently in order to ensure a continued, though slower, sense of achievements. Together with his compulsive drive for reform, achievement upon achievement, he generated in time the opposition of others who shared in the power of decision. This cycle tended to repeat itself in each of his three executive posts.

At Princeton, his demand for a graduate college based centrally on the campus ran into severe, prolonged opposition. There was considerable support for the proposed site for the graduate college favored by Andrew West, dean of the graduate school. The controversy lasted for several years and succeeded in dividing the Board of Trustees. To his wife Wilson complained that his difficulties were emerging in disturbing dreams. The complex series of events cannot be described here. Suffice it to say that they amply justified Arthur Link's conclusion cited above.

The Board of Trustees was finally able to come up with a compromise agreement that it fervently hoped would settle the matter. Wilson refused to accept its proposal. The matter was still hopelessly snarled when, unexpectedly, news came of a will that provided a bequest of several million dollars for construction of a graduate college and named Dean West as one of the executors of the will. Mrs. Wilson, it is said, heard her husband laughing when he was told of this development. "We have beaten the living," he said, "but we cannot fight the dead. The game is up." Wilson withdrew his objections to where the graduate college would be built.

By early June 1910, faced with defeat at Princeton, Wilson had an opportunity to extricate himself by running for governor of New Jersey. Wilson hoped to defer his resignation at Princeton until the election in New Jersey. But such was the animosity he had aroused that in October the trustees sent a delegation suggesting that he resign. One of the trustees was determined to make this private request a public demand should Wilson refuse. The next day Wilson presented a letter of resignation. Trustees accepted it immediately.

Later in his career, a situation of remarkable structural similarity arose. This was Wilson's struggle with Republican Senator Henry Cabot Lodge in which Lodge took the role of Dean West. In Wilson's struggle with Lodge, too, Wilson refused to compromise despite the fervent exertions of his friends as well as some of his opponents.

Wilson was locked in the same all-consuming battle with Lodge as earlier with West. He was driven to passionate stubbornness by the irresistible, never-articulated need to retaliate against the kind of domination he had endured as a child at the hands of his father. In the long-standing struggle with Lodge over ratification of the League of Nations, Wilson strove desperately to justify himself by demonstrating his moral superiority over his opponents. Becoming involved with Lodge, who despised Wilson, on this peculiarly personal level, Wilson refused compromising and brought a monumental defeat upon himself.

Did Wilson have insight into the personal sources of his stubbornness in his battles with West and Lodge? Typically, Wilson never attempted to probe into the sources of his personal makeup. But there are glimpses and some evidence that he was not totally unaware of the problem. We have already noted the nightmares during the Princeton imbroglio that he conveyed to his wife. During the early part of his presidency in Washington, Wilson spoke to Colonel Edward House, his close adviser, of nightmares in which he relived his struggles at Princeton. Wilson spoke anxiously, too, of the difficulty of maintaining during the last two years of his first term as president the level and pace of achievement he had accomplished in 1913–1914.[5]

There is also some evidence that Wilson was casting about for ways of avoiding a repetition of his highly distressing experience as a reformer at Princeton. For example, he cultivated the notion that with the passage of his impressive legislation program of 1913–1914 the task of reforming American economic life had been completed. Wilson publicly stated this in November 1914, which dismayed leaders of progressive opinion. The belief that he had already made his major political contribution suggests a rudimentary effort to protect himself—possibly through resignation or refusal of a second term—against the compulsive ambition that was creating anxiety.

My purpose in this chapter has been to utilize the pattern of Wilson's stubborn self-defeating behavior to illustrate the need for better criteria for employing counterfactual analysis to document "missed opportunities." More detailed analysis of Wilson's personal development and the role it played in his political behavior is available for interested readers.[6]

CHAPTER SIX
PREVENTION OF GENOCIDE:
THE WARNING-RESPONSE PROBLEM

(COAUTHORED WITH DAVID A. HAMBURG)

Genocide has occurred so often and so
uncontested in the last fifty years that an
epithet more apt in describing recent
events than the oft-chanted "Never
Again" is in fact "Again and Again."
—Samantha Power

This chapter draws on research underway in which we emphasize the need to create an *integrated warning-response system*, one that stresses the usability of early warning of possible genocide. Such a system does not exist today. Its major characteristics, however, can be identified. The creation of such a system will appreciably improve the ability of policymakers to make useful responses to *early warning* of genocide. This chapter also contains a proposal for creating one or more organizations devoted to prevention of genocide.

To be sure, early warning efforts themselves need to be improved. In addition, early warning must be brought more deliberately and effectively to the attention of important policymakers who decide what action to take.

We recognize the difficulties that impede policymakers' receptivity to early warning. They are numerous and not easily overcome. First, we note experimental research on factors that impede receptivity to warning. The results of these important laboratory studies, it will be seen, do not encourage hopes for an easy or complete solution to this problem.

Studies of an individual's ability to recognize an authentic warning indicator imbedded in a stream of other stimuli have shown at least three factors to be important:

1. The signal-to-noise ratio—that is, the strength of the signal (warning indicator) relative to the strength of confusing or distracting background stimuli

2. The expectations of observers called upon to evaluate such signals

3. The rewards and costs associated with recognizing and correctly appraising the signal

One might expect that the stronger the signal (warning indicator) and the weaker the background "noise," the easier it should be to detect the signal. However, laboratory experiments indicate that the detection of a signal is not simply a function of its strength relative to background "noise." In fact, the effect of a signal's strength on the ability to identify it can be less important than the second and third variables mentioned above.

A decisionmaker's *expectations*, as well as the *rewards and costs* associated with whether to recognize a signal, are often more important in determining receptivity to and correct appraisal of information about an emerging threat. These experimental findings are entirely consistent with what is known about how these factors operate in real-life situations to diminish receptivity to warning indicators of possible genocide. The "reward-cost" aspect of correct signal detection can sharply reduce policymakers' receptivity to new warning indicators.

Available data strongly support the proposition that *early warning does not necessarily make for any or an easy response.* On the contrary, policymakers often respond to new information about possible genocide by ignoring or downplaying it. It is well known from psychological studies that new information that calls into question an individual or organization's existing expectations is often required to meet higher standards of evidence than new information that supports existing expectations and policies. Top decisionmakers are typically reluctant to reopen existing policies unless absolutely necessary. Taking available warning seriously always carries the penalty of deciding what to do about it.

The foregoing discussion of receptivity to warning has been kept brief. It identifies impediments that cannot easily be eliminated. For this reason, we urge that *the task of securing warning should be linked closely with the problem of deciding what responses are appropriate, however equivocal or ambiguous that warning may be. This is the case we make for an integrated warning-response system.*

History teaches that two indicators constitute virtually unmistakable signs of genocide in preparation. One is the "demonization" of a group by a state's leaders; the other is governmentally supported "incitement" against the targeted group. Every modern case of genocide has been preceded by a mass media campaign by the government employing demonization and incitement against the targeted group. The presence of these two indicators indicates that the process of genocide is well underway. The implications for prompt responses to head it off are unmistakable.

There are, however, lesser portents of potential genocide—which we refer to as "*early* warning"—that also provide valuable opportunities for responses to discourage further moves toward genocide.

Although high confidence in early warning is desirable, often it is not available. But neither is it necessary for making useful responses to developments that may be moving toward genocide. Policymakers must become accustomed to taking early warning seriously, even if it is sometimes ambiguous or equivocal, or the likelihood of its eventuating in genocide remains uncertain.

We turn now to a discussion of better uses of available *early* warning. To be sure, some responses to it could be quite harmful. Required are well-considered responses that are useful in a given situation without posing the danger of unacceptable or undesired costs. However, even ambiguous or uncertain early warning gives policymakers more time to consider what to do, perhaps merely to undertake efforts to acquire better information about an evolving situation. Or to rehearse the decision problem they may face later, or to better assess the consequence if the initial warning proves to be credible and action-worthy. Early warning also provides an opportunity to review or create commitments and contingency plans. Even ambiguous early warning provides an opportunity to prepare to deal with an evolving conflict situation before it leads to genocide. In sum, early warning gives decisionmakers time to decide what to do now and/or to make preparations for possible action later.

Reference has already been made to the fact that efforts at "demonization" and "incitement" against the targeted group indicate advanced preparations and organization for undertaking genocide. A list of useful possible responses to *early* warning can also be provided. These response options will be listed without attempting to judge their utility in specific situations, a task that policymakers must decide.

1. Gather more information, both public and intelligence-based, about the situation.
2. Establish clear and reliable channels for communication, and engage in sustained dialogue with the leaders of the state in danger of genocide.
3. Governments and/or intergovernmental organizations can increase readiness and standby forces, and alert special forces for contingency operations.
4. Commitments to prevent genocide can usefully be reinforced by public statements as well as by private diplomacy.
5. Take measures to reduce unnecessary political/ diplomatic/economic costs that might result from the emerging crisis.
6. Consult with key states and allies, especially those with a deep moral commitment. Raise the issue in the United Nations and in other international bodies that have preventive capability.
7. Undertake a public information campaign to inform populations everywhere of the situa-

tion and prepare them for the possibility of coercive diplomatic, military-action, or other responses.

8. Conduct a decision rehearsal that assesses the damage to important interests and anticipates the political and psychological pressures policymakers are likely to feel should the crisis actually erupt. In addition, consider what can be done to mitigate the damage.

9. Clarify the commitment to act preventively if the threat of genocide is growing. Warning of genocide can stimulate policymakers to identify and assess the interests that a growing crisis jeopardizes. Such a review allows disentangling peripheral and negotiable issues from those that are central.

10. Review, update, and rehearse existing contingency plans. Improvise new policy options tailored to the emerging crisis, taking into account potential actions of other interested states and international organizations.

11. Initiate formal negotiations or mediation, bringing to bear all the strengths of preventive diplomacy. Help the parties to see the profound dangers of the genocidal path and the opportunities offered by other paths. Create a case for coexistence and, if possible, eventual reconciliation for mutual benefit.

We emphasize the need for an explicit effort to plan various responses to likely developments *before* they occur, and to associate particular options more closely with foreseeable cues. Of crucial importance is the need to consider warning always in conjunction with possible *responses* appropriate to different levels of urgent warning. Thus, genocide prevention requires a variety of response options related to different sorts of warning—options that spell out what can and should be done, by whom, in response to different kinds of warnings that genocide is probably on the horizon.

Important high-level initiatives have emphasized the need to fix responsibility for genocide prevention in existing or new organizations devoted to this goal. A strong impetus toward genocide prevention came from the January 2004 Stockholm International Forum on Genocide, sponsored by the Swedish government, long a committed leader in emphasizing this problem. On January 26, 2004, in the opening address to the Stockholm Forum, UN Secretary-General Kofi Annan affirmed that

> [t]here can be no more important issue, and no more binding obligation, than the prevention of genocide. Indeed, this may be considered one of the original purposes of the United Nations. . . . States [that are] parties to the Genocide Convention should consider setting up a Committee on the Prevention of Genocide, which would meet periodically to review reports and make recommendations for action.[1]

On January 28, Javier Solana, European Union (EU) High Representative for the Common Foreign and Security Policy, concluded the Stockholm Forum with these words:

> Our task now is to bring this work forward in our governments, institutions and organizations. . . . In the European Union . . . prevention . . . is at the heart of our approach to security . . . A culture of prevention requires the imagination to see ahead to the consequences of our inaction. And it demands the political will and courage to take preventive action where this is costly, dangerous or unpopular and where the benefits may never be seen.[2]

To achieve the goal expressed by Kofi Annan and Javier Solana, governments and international organizations will have to be alerted, prepared, and ready to undertake appropriate response at every stage. Indeed, efficacy in genocide prevention could be greatly enhanced by an international center established for this specific purpose in a strong institution and a set of cooperating governments. An international center for genocide prevention would collect appropriate staff, advisory groups, and a governing body, and build a network of relationships to mobilize the requisite knowledge and skill to meet the immense challenges of this historic mission. It would include a well-designed integrated warning-response system, as proposed in this chapter.

The international community stands warned. Ignorance is no longer a viable excuse for inaction. The twentieth-century genocides gave ample warning of the path to genocide. The years required to go from initial jeopardy to full genocide offer an interval in which the international community—if it is alert, well informed, morally committed, and organizationally prepared—can take preventive actions.

# NOTES

## Chapter 1

1. I have drawn on the useful discussion of ideology in Chapter 1 of R. M. Christenson, A. S. Engel, D. N. Jacobs, M. Ryan, and H. Waltser, *Ideologies and Modern Politics* (New York: Dodd, Mead, 1971). These authors, in turn, draw on a number of previous writers including Carl J. Friedrich and Andrew Hacker.

2. For an incisive critical analysis of the scientific and theoretical limitations of the concept of national interest, particularly as employed in classical Realist writings, see J. N. Rosenau, "National Interest," *International Encyclopedia of the Social Sciences,* Vol. 2.

3. This and the next few paragraphs draw on A. L. George, *Presidential Decisionmaking in Foreign Policy: The Effective Use of Information and Advice* (Boulder, CO: Westview Press, 1980), pp. 218–220.

4. Cf. J. G. March and H. A. Simon, *Organizations* (New York: John Wiley, 1958), pp. 156–157.

5. While all three values are fundamental, situations arise in which policymakers experience a trade-off dilemma among them—for example, between optimizing security and enhancing economic

well-being, or between optimizing security and maintaining one's way of life. See George, *Presidential Decisionmaking*, pp. 224–227, which draws on the treatment of this problem in S. Brown, *The Faces of Power* (New York: Columbia University Press, 1968), Part 1.

## Chapter 2

Research for Chapter 2 was supported by a grant (number SOC 75-14079) from the National Science Foundation and by the Center for Advanced Study in the Behavioral Sciences at which the author was a Fellow in 1976–1977. Parts of the chapter were presented earlier in a paper delivered to the Symposium on U.S. Foreign Policy in the Next Decade at the University of Missouri–Saint Louis, April 1977, and in a paper for a conference on approaches to the study of decisionmaking at the Norwegian Institute of International Affairs, Oslo, Norway, August 1977.

1. In preparing the interpretative essay on which this chapter is based, I relied mostly upon secondary sources describing Roosevelt's plans for a postwar security system and the Nixon-Kissinger détente policy. The case study of the détente policy is omitted from the chapter itself.

Roosevelt's "Great Design" for the postwar period was conveyed by him most explicitly in background interviews with Forrest Davis, who published detailed accounts of Roosevelt's plans and the beliefs supporting them in several articles appearing in the *Saturday Evening Post:* "Roosevelt's World Blueprint," 10 April 1943; "What Really Happened at Teheran—I," 13 May 1944; "What Really Happened at Teheran—II," 20 May 1944. [For background and evidence of Roosevelt's later acknowledgment that

Davis's articles accurately reflected his views, see John Lewis Gaddis, *The United States and the Origins of the Cold War* (New York: Columbia University Press, 1972), pp. 6, 153.] Detailed secondary accounts of Roosevelt's thinking and plans are to be found in Willard Range, *Franklin D. Roosevelt's World Order* (Athens: University of Georgia Press, 1959); Roland N. Stromberg, *Collective Security and American Foreign Policy* (New York: Praeger Publishers, 1963), esp. chap. 8; Robert A. Divine, *Roosevelt and World War II* (Baltimore, MD: Johns Hopkins University Press, 1969); Gaddis, *Origins of the Cold War;* Daniel Yergin, *Shattered Peace* (Boston: Houghton Mifflin Co., 1977), esp. chap. 2; and Robert Garson, "The Atlantic Alliance, Eastern Europe and the Origins of the Cold War: From Pearl Harbor to Yalta," in H. C. Allen and Roger Thompson, eds., *Contrast and Connection* (Columbus: Ohio State University Press, 1976), pp. 296–319.

2. The concept of "policy legitimacy" (versus "regime legitimacy") is discussed in a stimulating and insightful way by B. Thomas Trout, "Rhetoric Revisited: Political Legitimation and the Cold War," *International Studies Quarterly* 19, no. 3 (September 1975).

3. This important refinement of the analytical framework will not be developed further here since it will not be utilized in the case study.

4. Forrest Davis, "Roosevelt's World Blueprint," *Saturday Evening Post*, 10 April 1943. That the State Department was not an "ideological monolith" in its attitude toward the Soviet Union during and immediately after World War II has been persuasively argued and documented in recent studies. [Cf., for example, Robert L. Messer, "Paths Not Taken: The United States Department of State and Alternatives to Containment, 1945–1946," *Diplomatic History* 1 (Fall 1977).] Moreover, as Eduard Mark demonstrates,

Charles Bohlen and other State Department specialists did not operate on the assumption that there was an ineluctable conflict between the principle of self-determination in Eastern Europe and legitimate Soviet security interests in that area. Instead, they distinguished between different kinds of spheres of influence, arguing that an "open" (versus an "exclusive") Soviet sphere of influence in Eastern Europe was acceptable to and consistent with U.S. interests. See Mark's "Charles E. Bohlen and the Acceptable Limits of Soviet Hegemony in Eastern Europe. A Memorandum of 18 October 1945," *Diplomatic History* 2 (Spring 1979). On this point see also Thomas G. Patterson, *On Every Front: The Making of the Cold War* (New York: W. W. Norton & Co., 1979), chap. 3.

    5. Gaddis, *Origins of the Cold War*, pp. 198–205.

## Chapter 3

This chapter is based on a foreword I wrote for *Stable Peace Among Nations*, edited by Arie Kacowicz, Yaacov Bar-Siman-Tov, Ole Elgstrom, and Magnus Jerneck (Lanham, MD: Rowman and Littlefield, 2000). Their book is a unique contribution to the phenomenon of stable peace. Scholars from Sweden and Israel collaborated to produce the book. They also drew on contributions from other scholars. Included in their book are a number of excellent case studies of the development of stable peace in several countries. A chapter by Magnus Ericson discusses the relationship of stable peace to the democratic peace literature, a relationship that I develop further in the present chapter.

    1. "From Conflict to Peace: Stages Along the Road," *United States Institute of Peace Journal* 5, no. 6 (December 1992), pp. 7–9.

2. Karl W. Deutsch et al., *Political Community and the North Atlantic Area: International Organization in the Light of Historical Experience* (Princeton, NJ: Princeton University Press, 1957).

3. Kenneth E. Boulding, *Stable Peace* (Austin: University of Texas Press, 1978), p. 13.

4. In particular, see Raymond E. Lindgren, *Norway-Sweden: Disunion, and Scandinavian Integration* (Princeton, NJ: Princeton University Press, 1959); Bruce M. Russett, *Community and Contention: Britain and America in the Twentieth Century* (Westport, CT: Greenwood Press, 1963); Peter J. Katzenstein, *Disjoined Partners: Austria and Germany Since 1815* (Berkeley and Los Angeles: University of California Press, 1976).

5. Emanuel Adler and Michael Barnett, *Security Communities* (Cambridge, UK: Cambridge University Press, 1998).

6. Stephen R. Rock, *Why Peace Breaks Out* (Chapel Hill: University of North Carolina Press, 1989).

7. Erik Yesson, "Sovereignty, Domestic Politics, and Stable Peace," revised version of a paper presented at the Annual Meeting of the American Political Science Association, Chicago, 1995.

8. Stephen Rock, *Appeasement in International Politics* (Lexington: University Press of Kentucky, 2000).

9. See, for example, Roy F. Willis, *France, Germany, and the New Europe, 1945–1963* (Stanford, CA: Stanford University Press, 1965).

## Chapter 4

An earlier version of this chapter was published in Stanley R. Renshon and Deborah Larson, eds., *Good Judgment in Foreign Policy: Theory and Applications* (Lanham, MD: Rowman and Littlefield, 2003). The chapter also draws from previously published materials in

A. L. George, *Bridging the Gap: Theory and Practice in Foreign Policy* (Washington, DC: U.S. Institute of Peace, 1993), pp. 19–29; and A. L. George, "Analysis and Judgment in Policymaking," in , Kenneth J. Arrow et al., eds., *Education in a Research University* (Stanford, CA: Stanford University Press, 1996). The author expresses appreciation to the Carnegie Corporation of New York for research funds and to Kenneth Arrow, Philip Zelikow, and Deborah Welch Larson for helpful comments. In a personal communication, Herman Leonard, academic dean for teaching programs at the Kennedy School of Government, Harvard University, provided information on how the relationship between analysis and judgment is conceptualized and taught at the Kennedy School (Herman Leonard, letter to author, August 10, 1994). Paul Brest, then dean of the law school, Stanford University, provided material from a seminar he teaches that touches on problems of judgment.

1. For a more detailed discussion, see George, *Presidential Decisionmaking,* introduction and chap. 2. The latter considers various ways in which decisionmakers cope with uncertainty, including the use of either psychological coping devices or analytical methods for reducing the stress created by the need to make important decisions in the face of the limits on cognitive rationality and the presence of value complexity.

## Chapter 5

1. See, for example, the discussion in Abraham Kaplan, *Conduct of Inquiry* (Somerset, NJ: Transaction Publishers, 1998), pp. 21, 91, 160. A pioneering study that did much to stimulate thinking about counterfactuals was published by James D. Fearon, "Counterfactuals

and Hypothesis Testing in Political Science," *World Politics* 43, no. 2 (January 1991), pp. 169–195.

2. An important effort to see whether such standards could be identified and applied is Philip E. Tetlock and Aaron Belkin, eds., *Counterfactual Thought Experiments in World Politics* (Princeton, NJ: Princeton University Press, 1990). Tetlock and Belkin, and most of the contributors to the volume, took a sober view regarding the difficulty of formulating plausible counterfactuals. At one point, the editors state that "we seem to be stuck with quite literally a third-rate method" (p. 32). They highlight difficult-to-meet criteria for valid counterfactuals and urge analysts to be clearer and stricter in efforts to employ counterfactuals. See also Deborah Larson's study of missed opportunities during the U.S.-Soviet cold war: *Anatomy of Distrust: U.S.-Soviet Relations During the Cold War* (Ithaca, NY: Cornell University Press, 1997). And, particularly, Bruce Jentleson's effort to develop and apply strict criteria in the book he edited: *Opportunities Missed, Opportunities Seized: Preventive Diplomacy in the Post–Cold War World* (Lanham, MD: Rowman and Littlefield, 2000).

3. A. L. George and J. L. George, *Woodrow Wilson and Colonel House: A Personality Study* (New York: Dover Publications, 1964), p. 210. (The original version of this book was published by John Day in 1956.)

4. Arthur S. Link, *Wilson: The Road to the White House* (Princeton, NJ: Princeton University Press, 1947), pp. 90–91. A similar observation is made by historian John Morton Blum, *Woodrow Wilson and the Politics of Morality* (Boston: Scott Foresman, 1956), p. 36. Link later changed his 1947 analysis and subscribed instead to the assertion that Wilson's behavior on this and earlier occasions was due to a series of strokes.

5. Colonel House's diary entries 11/12/13, 12/22/13, 9/28/14 in the original House Diary. It was edited by Charles

Seymour, who left out of the published version of the Diary many critical reservations House made about Wilson. The expurgated version of the Diary is Charles Seymour, *The Intimate Papers of Colonel House*, 4 vols. (Boston and New York: Houghton Mifflin Co., 1926, 1928). The original House Diary is at Yale University.

6. George and George, *Woodrow Wilson and Colonel House;* A. L. George and J. L. George, *Presidential Personality and Performance* (Boulder, CO: Westview Press, 1998), esp. chap. 4, "Woodrow Wilson and Colonel House: A Reply to Weinstein, Anderson, and Link." A detailed analysis of the "compensation" hypothesis I have used to understand Wilson's development is presented in A. L. George, "Power as a Compensatory Value for Political Leaders," *Journal of Social Issues* 24, no. 3 (1968).

## Chapter 6

1. Address by UN Secretary-General Kofi Annan, in *Stockholm International Forum 2004: Preventing Genocide* (Stockholm: January 26–28, 2004), pp. 18–20.

2. EU High Representative Javier Solana, "Preventing Genocide: Threats and Responsibilities," speech delivered on January 28, 2004, at the Stockholm Conference on Genocide. Available online at http://europa-eu-un.org/articles/en/article_3176_en.htm; accessed February 12, 2005.

# APPENDIX ONE:
## CREDITS

## Chapter 1   Ideology, National Interest, and National Values

This chapter was written for this book. It draws selectively from seven pages (1–3, 8–14) of the author's twenty-one-page article "Ideology and International Relations: A Conceptual Analysis," *Jerusalem Journal of International Relations* 9, no. 1 (1987). This journal ceased publication in 1992.

## Chapter 2   The Need for Policy Legitimacy

This chapter was prepared for this book. It draws from pages 233–251 and 258–260 of the author's twenty-one-page article "Domestic Constraints on Regime Change in U.S. Foreign Policy: The Need for Policy Legitimacy" in *Changes in the International System,* edited by Ole R. Holsti, Randolph Siverson, and Alexander L. George (Boulder, CO: Westview Press, 1980). Left out of this chapter is the case study of the Nixon-Kissinger détente policy.

## Chapter 3  Stable Peace and Democratic Peace

This chapter reproduces with minor changes the author's brief foreword to *Stable Peace Among Nations,* edited by A. M. Kacowicz, Y. Bar-Siman-Tov, O. Elgstrom, and Magnus Jerneck (Lanham, MD: Rowman and Littlefield, 2000) (published originally as "Democracy and Peace" in *Scandinavian Political Studies* 23, no. 3, 2000).

## Chapter 4  Analysis and Judgment

This chapter reproduces with minor changes the author's article "Analysis and Judgment in Policymaking," which appeared in *Education in a Research University* (pp. 343–350), edited by Kenneth J. Arrow, Richard W. Cottle, B. Curtis Eaves, and Ingram Olkin (Stanford, CA: Stanford University Press, 1996). Copyright © 1996 by the Board of Trustees of the Leland Stanford Jr. University. All rights reserved. Used with the permission of Stanford University Press, www.sup.org.

## Chapter 5  The Role of Counterfactuals in "Missed Opportunities"

This original piece was written for this book. It draws selectively from eight pages (43, 45, 52, 285, 290–291, 370–371) in A. L. George and J. L. George, *Woodrow Wilson and Colonel House: A Personality Study,* originally published by John Day Company in 1956 and reproduced by Dover Publications in 1964.

## Chapter 6  Prevention of Genocide:
## The Warning-Response Problem

This chapter draws on research being prepared by David A. Hamburg and Alexander L. George.

# APPENDIX TWO:
# SELECTED WORKS
# OF ALEXANDER L. GEORGE

1956    *Woodrow Wilson and Colonel House: A Personality Study.*
        With Juliette L. George. New York: John Day.

1959    *Propaganda Analysis: A Study of Inferences Made from Nazi
        Propaganda in World War II.* Evanston, IL: Row, Peterson.

1967    *The Chinese Communist Army in Action: The Korean War
        and Its Aftermath.* New York: Columbia University Press.

1971    *The Limits of Coercive Diplomacy: Laos, Cuba, Vietnam.*
        With David K. Hall and William E. Simons. Boston:
        Little, Brown.

1974    *Deterrence in American Foreign Policy: Theory and Practice.*
        With Richard Smoke. New York: Columbia University
        Press.

1976    *Towards a More Soundly Based Foreign Policy: Making Better
        Use of Information.* App. 2. Commission on the
        Organization of the Government for the Conduct of

Foreign Policy. Washington, DC: U.S. Government Printing Office.

1980   *Presidential Decisionmaking in Foreign Policy: The Effective Use of Information and Advice.* Boulder, CO: Westview Press.

1983   *Managing U.S.–Soviet Rivalry: Problems of Crisis Prevention.* Boulder, CO: Westview Press.

1983   *Force and Statecraft: Diplomatic Problems of Our Time.* With Gordon A. Craig. New York: Oxford University Press.

1988   *U.S.–Soviet Security Cooperation: Achievements, Failures, Lessons.* Ed. with Philip J. Farley and Alexander Dallin. New York: Oxford University Press.

1991   *Avoiding War: Problems of Crisis Management.* Boulder, CO: Westview Press.

1992   *Forceful Persuasion: Coercive Diplomacy as an Alternative to War.* Washington, DC: U.S. Institute of Peace.

1993   *Bridging the Gap: Theory and Practice in Foreign Policy.* Washington, DC: U.S. Institute of Peace.

1994   *Limits of Coercive Diplomacy*, expanded 2d ed. With William E. Simons. Boulder, CO: Westview Press.

1997   *Preventing Deadly Conflict.* Final report, Carnegie Commission on Preventing Deadly Conflict. New York.

1998   *Presidential Personality and Performance.* With Juliette L. George. New York: Perseus Books.

2005   *Case Studies and Theory Development in the Social Sciences.* With Andrew Bennett. Cambridge, MA: MIT Press.

# INDEX

# ABOUT THE AUTHOR

Alexander L. George is the Graham H. Stuart Professor of International Relations Emeritus at Stanford University. He was an analyst and department head at the RAND Corporation from 1948 to 1968. He has been at Stanford since 1968, where, in addition to courses on international relations, he taught seminars on decision-making, political leadership, and the presidency. He won the Bancroft Prize in 1975 for *Deterrence in American Foreign Policy* (New York: Columbia University Press, 1974), and was awarded a five-year MacArthur Foundation Prize Fellowship in 1983. From 1994 to 1999 he served on the Carnegie Commission on Preventing Deadly Conflict and from 1995 to 1999 as chair of the Committee on Conflict Resolution at the National Academy of Sciences. In 1997, the National Academy of Sciences conferred on him its Award for Behavioral Research Relevant to the Prevention of Nuclear War. Currently, with David Hamburg, he is working on the problem of preventing genocide.